The Secrets Are Out

Nothing Happens Until the Secrets Are Revealed!

Surely the Lord God will do nothing but he revealeth his secret until his servants the prophets.
— Amos 3:7

Lady Mary Hatter

© Copyright 2017, Lady Mary Hatter

All Rights Reserved.

No part of this book may be reproduced or transmitted in any form or by any means, electronic or mechanical, including photocopying, recording or by any information storage and retrieval system, without the written permission of the Publisher, except where permitted by law.

ISBN: 978-1-60414-951-7

Published by Mary Hatter
Spring, Texas 77373

Cover Design / Creation by Mary Hatter

Unless otherwise noted, all Scripture references are from the King James Version of the Bible. 1972, 1976, 1979, 1983, 1984 1985 Thomas Nelson Inc. Publishers.

Contents

Introduction 5
Dedication and Acknowledgements 9
November 2015 11
November 7, 2015 11
January 2016 13
February 22
March 28
April 41
May 54
June 64
July 74
August 81
September 89
October 99
November 105
December 107
Conclusion 118
About the Author 121
Bonus Content 123

Introduction

I'm so blessed! I'm so amazed! Gods Word is true! Look at what He's chosen to do! He's blessed me and He's blessed you! God has done it again! I'm grateful for all He's done by grace through faith. He continues to make a way. To all that will hear, listen, and do: God has spoken, is speaking and will continue to speak to you. He's allowed His secrets to come out, so that the blessings will come about. Shout. In this book, **The Secrets Are Out**, you will hear what to do, your job is to follow through. See what God says in this scripture:

> *Surely the Lord God will do nothing without revealing His secret to His servants the prophets. [Rev. 10:7.]*
>
> Amos 3:7 AMPC

I thank God for choosing me to serve Him and His people. My prayer to the unsaved as you read is that you will come to know Him indeed. Please confess this with me, and you shall receive. Say this out loud. God I acknowledge that Jesus is my Lord. I believe in my heart that he died and was raised from the dead. Come into my heart now. I receive You as Lord and savior of my life. Thank You God for saving me.

> *Because if you acknowledge and confess with your lips that Jesus is Lord and in your heart believe (adhere to,*

> *trust in, and rely on the truth) that God raised Him from the dead, you will be saved.*
>
> Romans 10:9 AMPC

Now that you are saved, continue and hear what God is saying to His church. Get this scripture in your heart. God will never depart. Always obey, what He has to say, and the blessings shall continue to come your way everyday.

> *Anyone with ears to hear must listen to the Spirit and understand what he is saying to the churches.*
>
> Revelation 2:29 NLT

This book is powerful. Why? Because God has spoken by way of Holy Spirit through me. Nothing happens except the secrets are revealed, spoken, and received. Know that God wants you to have the best. As His children, you are far greater than the rest. He's allowed you to show off in Him.

God gets all the glory and praise. I bless His Holy name. His name never changes; He's always the same. Our hope is in Christ Jesus. We are blessed for this very reason. This is our season.

His Kingdom shall continue to reign, in Jesus' name. There is no other name greater. Again, hear, listen, and do as I speak to you. Know who Holy Spirit speaks through. As this year of 2017 approaches, hear what God has spoken.

God spoke these words. "Staying Clean and Receiving Everything in 2017." What an awesome God! Will you receive? I receive.

Continue to pray, and praise Him. As I write, I can hardly wait for you to receive, what God has spoken to me. *The Secrets Are Out* will bless His people and all those who will obey what He has said, is saying, and continues to say. It's a must that we obey. God's Word spoken will help fix the broken. See what He says in this scripture:

> *The Spirit of the Lord is upon me, because he hath anointed me to preach the gospel to the poor; he hath*

sent me to heal the brokenhearted, to preach deliverance to the captives, and recovering of sight to the blind, to set at liberty them that are bruised,

Luke 4:18 KJV

I know you will be blessed. This is why: God has already done it by grace, through faith. Continue to read on. Speak what He says. Love Him with all your might, your mind, and live right all the time. Make sure your motive is love, in all you do. Know that He first loved you. You are His beloved ones. He has displayed His love, in giving you His only begotten son. The victory overall has been won. Be blessed. Enjoy!

Dedication and Acknowledgements

To my husband, Pastor A.D. Hatter, my two children, Tangeneva and Tristian. My granddaughter, Maranda, and another grandchild that's coming from my daughter, Tangeneva. I love you all dearly.

I also dedicate this book to those who are ready and willing to hear what God has revealed, and continues to reveal to His prophet by way of Holy Ghost. To those who are reading and don't understand right now, this book is dedicated to you also.

To all who read, I speak blessings to you indeed. This is my seed. I sow, as you will grow and go, and the people will know. I speak continual blessings to the kingdom, and many souls being saved. Blessings, blessings, and blessings always!

November 2015

NOVEMBER 7, 2015

Regardless of what you think a person is, or what they're not doing, God has already done it. Watch the negative words you speak because you can't take them back. Don't listen to negative words that others speak because they get inside your mind and they will come up again.

> *These things I have spoken unto you, that in me ye might have peace. In the world ye shall have tribulation: but be of good cheer; I have overcome the world.*
>
> John 16:33 KJV

Death and life is in the power of YOUR tongue not no one else's. What you speak is from you, and what others speak is from them, therefore no one can speak death on you, and God allows it to happen just because they spoke it. You choose the blessings not the curses, not others choose. Continue to speak what Holy Spirit speaks through you, not what you want, or what others speak for you, or to you. Make sure your words build up and not tear down. A froward mouth God frowns.

> *Put away from thee a froward mouth, and perverse lips put far from thee.*
>
> Proverbs 4:24 KJV

> *Liars hate their victims; flatterers sabotage trust.*
>
> Proverbs 26:28 MSG

> *They must not slander anyone and must avoid quarreling. Instead, they should be gentle and show true humility to everyone.*
>
> Titus 3:2 NLT

> *I say this in order that no one may mislead and delude you by plausible and persuasive and attractive arguments and beguiling speech.*
>
> Colossians 2:4 AMP

> *Now I beseech you, brethren, mark them which cause divisions and offenses contrary to the doctrine which ye have learned; and avoid them.*
>
> Romans 16:17 KJV

God reveals, exposes, and removes every word spoken, and anything that didn't come from Him when we ask.

> *Ask it shall be given, Seek and you shall find, Knock and the door shall be opened unto you.*
>
> *Keep on asking, and you will receive what you ask for. Keep on seeking, and you will find. Keep on knocking, and the door will be opened to you.*
>
> Matthew 7:7-8 NLT

This is a continual *process* to receive continual *progress*, and all *promotions*, *provisions*, and *prosperity* from almighty all powerful God. He blesses the fruit of your lips with peace, and healing.

I create the fruit of the lips; Peace, peace to him that is far off, and to him that is near, saith the Lord; and I will heal him.

Isaiah 57:19

Never forsake to speak God's Word in season and out of season, always have a speaking spirit that only comes from God.

January 2016

JANUARY 13, 2016

Lifetime Warranties

God has given me Lifetime Warranties of blessings that never run out. My seeds never stop coming and I never stop sowing. I say get out the way to lack; you can't stay. The blessings are on the way, today. I have more than enough, exceedingly, abundantly, above all that I could have asked or thought about. I'm on track. Enemy get back.

Worship is getting into God's presence allowing Him to speak through me, from the inside out, and receiving what God wants to get to me, through His Spirit. I'm continually receiving by grace through faith everything that God has allowed to come my way; and it's all here to stay.

He has opened doors like never before. I'm a receiver of the blessings. I'm living a great life of love and laughter. I'm abundantly supplied, and money is supernaturally multiplied.

God has allowed me to receive His love. He is rich in love, because He gave His only begotten son. The victory was won at the cross. *I'm redeemed, restored, resting, reigning, ruling, renewed, relying on, and receiving the riches* of the blood; that was shed for the remission of my sins.

In John 3:16 the key is He gave. For me the price was paid. What a wonderful time. I'm living in God's divine. The shine is on. My light never goes dark or dim; it's a continual light, as I continually *pray, praise, and receive His promises*. I worship God in spirit and in truth. I receive all that He wants me to do.

JANUARY 13, 2016

I receive my Divine promotions

Blow winds, blow! Monies that I didn't know! Blessings untold! Blessings unfolded! Blessings I behold! I'm like a tree planted by the rivers of water, I bring forth my fruit in my season; my leaf never wither; and whatsoever I do and have done, prospers. My leaves can never wither, because God has brought this all about. His prosperity never runs out.

As far as the east is from the west, God has allowed me to be His very best. I'm far greater than the rest, because I've passed the test. God, your Word, your wisdom, and your wealth, I will never forget. Thank you God for the **Wind Of Wealth**. **WOW!** I'm receiving it all now! I'm receiving and living in great health.

My divine promotions are taking place in my life today, and they are here to stay! I believe. I believe. I believe. I receive. I receive. I receive. The blessings of the Lord are on me. More, and more, and more, God has opened all the doors. The reign is here. God is sending people to help me.

Favor, favor, and favor, all without labor. I shall know who they are. They will say they are sent by God. This is the Lord's doing and it's marvelous in our sight. This is our season of supernatural surplus. God has done it for this very reason.

The kingdom of God is at hand. He is using man, and woman. We are all in His plans. It's all in our hands. Stand, you are not a fan. You are a friend of God, heirs and joint heirs with Christ Jesus. Know that blessings were preserved for this very reason.

The kingdom of God is at hand. Use what I've placed in your hands. I'm the almighty God and I'm always near, do what I allowed you to hear. I'm never far, and My Word never departs. Always keep My Word in your heart.

The break is on. Just like the fishermen's nets break, make no mistake, your nets break. It's all for My kingdom's sake, you are receiving for this very reason. Rejoice and be exceedingly glad. You are receiving overflowing and outpouring of blessings you never had. I'm the almighty God and if it wasn't so, I wouldn't have said it.

Remember I am the Lord, your God; I change not. Remember this day. All My exceedingly, abundantly, above all you could have every asked or thought about blessings, have come to you today; and make sure you allow them to stay. Stay steadfast, unmovable, always abounding in My Word and work.

Hear, listen, and do, everything, I've said, am saying, and shall continue to say to you. You know what to do, because the Spirit of the Lord is upon you. Continue to pray in the Holy Spirit, and this is how you shall live. All my revelations I shall reveal, and you shall continue to give.

JANUARY 14, 2016

BARCODE

God has given us a barcode to be scanned, pull up, read, and this is His daily Word. There's no price to pay because it has been paid through His Son, Jesus Christ, who died on the cross and rose again, for the remission of our sins.

Place your barcode on the counter of life. Everything that God allowed you to place on the counter, you will see, hear, listen, and do. Let your requests be made known unto God, put your barcode on the counter. It's scanned, God sees it, reads it, because it's the barcode He's given you; then He gives you what you have requested.

Be careful of the bad barcode that has to be typed in by man; this leaves room for human error. If just one number is wrong, you can't get your item you want in life — the items of grace and faith.

God has already given us by grace through faith every item on the counter available through the barcode presented, scanned, and read by God and released to you. Praise Him for all the things He's given us!

Barcodes are important, necessary, and need to be presented to receive the items. Make sure it's a good barcode, to be read by God and your items are received.

Make sure all your items are presented. If you leave some in the basket, then you are a thief and God didn't scan your items, He didn't read them and you could be prosecuted.

You have been chosen to receive God's barcode. Don't be like the enemy, who seeks those whom he may devour. He robs, steals, kills and destroys.

God has come and given you life and life more abundantly. Present your God-given barcode to have it scanned and read by Him, and receive the things He has already made available to you. Remember the items with barcodes have been sitting on the shelf waiting for you to pick them up, take them to the counter, scan, read it, check out.

Jesus paid the price, for you to receive your items of blessings. Hallelujah!!!

JANUARY 16, 2016

The dream of Divine Promotions we have received and are walking in daily

This dream was revealed from God. Apostle Thompson spoke over us that we would have dreams. He mentioned that "regardless of what the dream is, don't see it as bad and get scared, it's God revealing things to you and showing you what to do, so the blessings can be released to you."

This is the revelation of the dream from yesterday. My family is imparted, instructed, and infested with increase. The rain is here: we are flooding, and flowing in our finances. The rain came quickly. Our children and grandchild are here with us in this wealth and riches. Even through one of our children did things his own way; he is with us anyway.

As we float in our beds we are comfortably moving ahead: this is one of the reasons the blood was shed. There is no water coming over our heads. Even though one of the persons on my husband's side of the family laughed at and tried to stop our grandchild; she didn't respond and go with him.

As we are floating in our beds, we are enjoying ourselves and excited about what's ahead. This was like a river with no ending. There were no obstructions in our view. God is saying, "This is all for you."

We are enjoying the sail. We are Floating on. The victory has already been won. We have been *changed, cleansed, corrected and continue* to move higher, as we have been elevated in Christ Jesus. Our *position, promises, and promotions* came quickly, just like in this passage of scripture.

> *And suddenly there came a sound from heaven as of a rushing mighty wind, and it filled all the house where they were sitting. And there appeared unto them cloven tongues like as of fire, and it sat upon each of them. And they were all filled with the Holy Ghost, and began to speak with other tongues, as the Spirit gave them utterance.*
>
> Acts 2:2-4 KJV

We have been baptized in blessings of all kinds. This increase causes us to shine and walk in God's divine. Divine promotions are mine. We are receiving every time. Never falling out of the bed. Never worrying about what's ahead or anything people have said.

God is pleased, He has meet our needs, and given us the desires of our hearts. We got the power; this was not just a rain shower. The rain came quickly and flooded us while we were in our beds. I knew it was coming, because I heard God say, "Prepare for it," and I did.

I knew this day was coming, because Apostle Thompson spoke, "Divine promotions will take place in our lives in the next five days." I wrote this down and dated it.

I believe God's prophets, so I am prospering. I'm prospering not just in wealth, but also in health. The flooding of the water didn't drown us, and no one got out or fell out of bed. We just continued to enjoy the floating.

I shall continue to stay faithful as we flood and flow in finances. I receive all that God has and shall continue to give me. Blessings, blessings, blessings shall never cease, because the Spirit of the Lord is upon me. I'm free of debt, doubt, and drought.

My soul is free, there's no chains holding me down, I'm no longer bound. Praise the Lord; I'm free. Hallelujah! Hallelujah! Hallelujah! Thank you God!

JANUARY 21, 2016

The Network Marketing of the Kingdom!

As believers we are charged to carry out the Great Commission; which is found in this scripture.

> *And Jesus came and spake unto them, saying, All power is given unto me in heaven and in earth. Go ye therefore, and teach all nations, baptizing them in the name of the Father, and of the Son, and of the Holy Ghost: Teaching them to observe all things whatsoever I have commanded you: and, lo, I am with you always, even unto the end of the world. Amen.*
>
> Matthew 28:18-20 KJV

God has *chosen, charged, commissioned, and commanded* us to go: therefore we must win souls to the kingdom of God, which is at hand, and He has chosen to use man. When you witness and win one soul, then that soul is responsible for winning another soul, and so on. Each one should reach one, and the kingdom of God will continue to be built up.

We market God the father, His son Jesus Christ, Holy Spirit, and His angels: and the people will choose to receive or not receive them. We must know our products, and where to get our information. The bible is a great place to study and know what to say, and answer all mankind.

Holy Spirit gives us Divine Revelations from God. We speak and do things in Jesus' name. Our angels hearken to our voice and bring the souls in that we have called and commanded, minister to, and have a desire to come into the kingdom.

We must be always ready and willing to tell people about God. Always believing for the souls to come daily. This is a lifetime work of the ministry of Jesus Christ, you, and the body of Christ.

JANUARY 28, 2016

Poet/Prophetess! Proverbs 31:10-31

Seven Strengths Supernaturally Supplied from the Saviour!

        1) Promoter of Prosperity

        2) Praiser and Powerful

        3) Positioned to Prosper

        4) Possessing of Promises

        5) Full Of Holy Ghost

        6) Financial Overflow Harvest

        7) Faithful Obedient Holy

I'm flowing and growing in my gifts and callings. I'm anointed to speak and reach the masses. I teach the teachable and the unreachable. I reach beyond my reach, because the teacher is continuing to teach me.

I give what's been given me. Love, unconditionally. I love God with my whole heart, and nothing can pull me apart. I'm set apart. I've been made holy, as He is holy.

I have blessings, blessings, blessings; they are overflowing and overtaking me. The words I speak are not my own. I see what I see, teach what I teach, preach what I preach, because the Spirit of the Lord is upon me. I'm sure of my calling and election, therefore I never fail, because God has checked my mail.

I'm sealed, delivered, and there's no return to sender. *I'm sorted, searched, separated, sectioned, and secured* in the right package. I'm not damaged or dropped, however I'm delivered to the correct mailbox.

I have *divine dominion and destinations*. I speak to the unsaved, and they can't resist the words spoken from me by way of Holy Spirit. The unsaved must confess this scripture openly:

> *If you openly declare that Jesus is Lord and believe in your heart that God raised him from the dead, you will be saved. If you are unsaved, speak this now, and you are saved.*
>
> Romans 10:9 NLT

According to this scripture:

> *For Everyone who calls on the name of the LORD will be saved.*
>
> Romans 10:13 NLT

Let's go to places unknown. Follow the yellow brick road. Places untold, where wealth and riches unfold. I behold, Heaven right here on earth. I live in the kingdom, plenty promotions and promises, which have been preserved, and provided for you. It's all yours. It's your time. Walk in your divine promotions daily.

I spoke it through My prophets. You believed and you received. I'm pleased. Rejoice, and be exceedingly glad. Your future is better than your past. Your blessings shall always last. You are a walking wonder. Every place where the soles of your feet tread is yours.

You shall continue to grow and flow in your gifts and callings. You are more powerful than ever. You are not afraid of no devil. Speak My Word. Teach My Word. Reach the world. Live in <u>Health</u>, <u>Overflow</u>, and <u>Wealth</u>! This is **<u>HOW</u>** we do it! Your almighty, all-powerful God.

JANUARY 29, 2016

A mighty move of God! The move is on!

God has spoken. It's moving time. We are walking in God's divine. Holy Spirit has prompted me to call on the Angels. They are on assignment for us.

They are ministering and continue to minister to the board and members of our new church home.

I have called, commissioned, and commanded, the innumerable Angels to go, and they are on assignment for us now. They have heard the word from God, spoken from my mouth, to move on our behalf now. Release has taken place. The board and members have heard by way of Holy Spirit and the Angels have brought it to pass.

Pastor AD and I are the chosen of God to lead this church of thousands of members to the next level in the kingdom of God. They have turned from their way of thinking and heard from God by way of the ministering angels. We have heard from the prophets and now we are prospering and the kingdom is prospering because of our obedience and the people of God's obedience.

The move is on. We are moving into our new church and new property. We receive. The spirit of the Lord is upon me. We went through for a reason. We learned and have earned. We now have testimonies of times, places, and manifestation. Thank you, God, for this mighty move.

The wind has blown the doors open. Angels have come in. I receive my visitation and manifestation. This is a quick move. Demonstration has taken place, because we are a kingdom generation. Generations and generations to come. The move is on.

Victory, victory, victory, has been won. Thank God for His son. I'm never afraid, because this move, God has allowed to be made. God's not a man. It's all in his plans. He's placed it all in our hands. We follow the process and receive our positions.

God is pleased to prosper His people. Thank you, God, for this large place of promotion and promises. We never stress, struggle, or strain, because God has brought the reign. We are *resting, ruling, rendering, refreshed, restored, and receiving* it all for the kingdom's sake and for our sakes.

I see, I see, what God wants me to see. I hear, listen and do everything unto God. We never forget from where God has brought us.

We follow instructions. We have the impartation. Same grace as our mentors. Never missing a move or moment of our time, travels and destinations that have been set up for us by God. We are going far. This move has topped the bar.

No barrier blockers, instead there are bountiful blessings. Continue, continue, continue, all this has become new. "The blessings of the Lord are upon you." This says our almighty, all powerful God. These words I speak are not my own, but the One who owns. This heaven we are experiencing right here on earth.

I receive, I receive, I receive. Thank you God for the spirit of the Lord shall continue to be upon me. Thank God for the four winds of His Holy Spirit. I receive, all these: that were spoken in the scriptures.

> *Saying with a loud voice, Worthy is the Lamb that was slain to receive power, and riches, and wisdom, and strength, and honour, and glory, and blessing.*
>
> Revelation 5:12 KJV

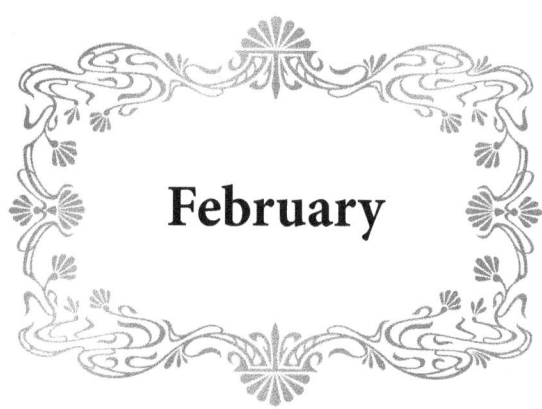

FEBRUARY 5, 2016

Pick It Up, Put It On: You Have Won!

Never put away what has been working for you because of a temporary light affliction that only lasts for a moment. Just know it's still working. The enemy has brought his people out in numbers and we must bring God's people out in more numbers. Pray continually, calling the Angels constantly. Believe what you pray according to the will of God has come to past. Never lacking, always packing with the power of God.

These are the times that allow us to move in dimensions of His Divine! "Shine, shine, shine, you are mine," says the Lord of hosts. I have put you on this post. For you, I have done the most. The vision for you has already been wrote.

Hear Me, listen, and do everything I have planned for you. This is My will for you. You have weathered the storm. The storm hasn't weathered you. You are in control. Even from the beginning, I have caused you to have dominion. You are a winner. You never loose, with what I given you to use. I have equipped you with these tools. Grace, and mercy, all through faith.

Keep it moving. There's no room for doom and gloom. The light is on. Shine in My Divine, because it's all Mine. The tracker is off. The enemy can't find you, because I've placed you under the shadow of My almighty wings. He's blinded because you are kingdom minded. My kingdom is at hand; continue to stand.

> *Put on all of God's armor so that you will be able to stand firm against all strategies of the devil. For we are not fighting against flesh-and-blood enemies, but against evil rulers and authorities of the unseen world, against mighty powers in this dark world, and against evil spirits in the heavenly places. Therefore, put on every piece of God's armor so you will be able to resist the enemy in the time of evil. Then after the battle you will still be standing firm. Stand your ground, putting on the belt of truth and the body armor of God's righteousness. For shoes, put on the peace that comes from the Good News so that you will be fully prepared. In addition to all of these, hold up the shield of faith to stop the fiery arrows of the devil. Put on salvation as your helmet, and take the sword of the Spirit, which is the word of God. Pray in the Spirit at all times and on every occasion. Stay alert and be persistent in your prayers for all believers everywhere. And pray for me,*

> *too. Ask God to give me the right words so I can boldly explain God's mysterious plan that the Good News is for Jews and Gentiles alike. I am in chains now, still preaching this message as God's ambassador. So pray that I will keep on speaking boldly for him, as I should.*
>
> Ephesians 6:11-20 NLT

This is how you make your moves, again, you never loose, with the tools I gave you to use. I love you unconditionally. "I am, that I am, I change not, I gave you everything you got." Praise Me in the good and the bad. Your good always outweighs the bad.

You have been brought out of the past. Keep pressing, even in the testing. The triumph is the finish up! Never quit, you are **FIT** — **F**aithful, **I**mportant, **T**rustworthy. Exercise your gifts and talents. Pump it up! Nothing is too heavy for you, because weights build you up.

> *Wherefore seeing we also are compassed about with so great a cloud of witnesses, let us lay aside every weight, and the sin which doth so easily beset us, and let us run with patience the race that is set before us, Looking unto Jesus the author and finisher of our faith; who for the joy that was set before him endured the cross, despising the shame, and is set down at the right hand of the throne of God.*
>
> (Hebrews 12:1-2)

You have **MUSCLES**. **M**anifestations, **U**nlimited **S**upply, **C**ontinually **L**oving, **E**xercising **S**upernaturally. I am always with you. I never leave or forsake you. I have unconditional love for you. I am the almighty, all-powerful God. I speak what has already been worked out for you. Hear, listen, and do.

FEBRUARY 6, 2016

The ball is in your court!

The playing field is leveled. You have power over the devil. You must play to win. Never be bound in sin. I have given you life again. You must work for Me without hindrances.

I have raised you up. I have brought you out, have no doubt. I'm moving in every situation in your life. Pray without ceasing. Praise without ceasing. You are alive for this very reason.

I spared you to bring you out. You are out of darkness of the world that you thought was about you and yours. The doors are open, enter into My place of *rescue, rest, redemption, restoration, righteousness, refreshing, and receive* all My wonderful things I set up for you. Why? Because I love you and I trust you to serve Me wholeheartedly.

You are My example in the earth. I give you the *fullness, fruitfulness, and fatness* of this earth. You have *overflowing, outpouring, and overtaking* of finances. You need this for My kingdom's sake. I make no mistake.

Throw the ball. Run the play. I have made the way. Just because you didn't come in first, don't mean you didn't win the race. It's the finishing that counts in My book. This lamb's book of life, which your name is written in.

I have made good on My promises. What I've spoken has come to pass. Don't forget you have teammates. This is so for My sake. I am your almighty God.

I'm never far. I'm always there with you. Hear, listen, and do, because I got you. Again you are out. Don't forget to shout. Remember I brought this all about. Love, inspite of hardship. I have set you above the rest. You are My very best. Enjoy!!!

FEBRUARY 12, 2016

Catch us, Lord. Hide us under the shadow of Your wings. We never fail or fall because we are *imparted, inspired, and instructed* in God's Word. We obey and serve because we are set apart, and love God with all our hearts.

We continue to *confess, command, and continue* to pray without *ceasing*. We are chosen and commissioned to go everywhere and teach, and tell people about what He has already done. He shall continue to work in, and through us.

We are living under and open heaven. We have the supply of heaven. We are on the path of perpetual increase. Increase is in our hands. We are being used by God and given things from Him, coming through man.

Holy Ghost allows us to have the *most, the mind, and the manifestations,* that only come from God. Angels are always on assignment, making sure all our promises are received for what has been given us from God. Know that God is speaking even when we are not listening and learning. Know that God is working even when we are slothful and sleeping.

> *For we are God's [own] handiwork (His workmanship), recreated in Christ Jesus, [born anew] that we may do those good works which God predestined (planned beforehand) for us [taking paths which He prepared ahead of time], that we should walk in them [living the good life which He prearranged and made ready for us to live].*
>
> Ephesians 2:10 AMP

FEBRUARY 17, 2016

Pray to God without ceasing. Praise Him for this very reason. This is our season. The kingdom of God is at hand. God is using man and woman. Everything is in our hands. In the evil days, we must stand.

When the enemy tries to shut you out, remember you are never left without. The earth is the Lord's and the fullness thereof, and they that dwell there in. You never lose; you always win. Never be bound by sin.

When the world is having parties, and Christians are mixing in; remember to stay dressed with the whole armor of God and stand in the evil days. Christians are funding the world's system and leaving the kingdom of God in lack. As believers we know this is how the enemy attacks.

We must speak God's Word in season and out of season; this is how we fight back. God shall always keep us on track, and we will never lack. We want for nothing, as we continue to love, obey, hear, listen and do everything God has already spoken for us to do.

We are *divinely directed, delivered, dominating, subduing, replenishing, and multiplying,* in this earth. We are God's creation, as we have already been given supernatural manifestation. Believers must take charge and control over nations. This is the Word from God spoken in this scripture.

> *So God created man in his own image, in the image of God created he him; male and female created he them. And God blessed them, and God said unto them, Be fruitful, and multiply, and replenish the earth, and subdue it: and have dominion over the fish of the sea, and over the fowl of the air, and over every living thing that moveth upon the earth.*
>
> Genesis 1:27-28 KJV

FEBRUARY 22, 2016

In your dark circles there is always light that is surrounding you and outshining the darkness. The stars always out number and shine bright in the dark skies. You never have to worry about your dark days because Jesus is the light that always outshines darkness: whatever darkness you face.

In the middle of adversity light continues to shine. "You are walking in My favor," says your almighty, all powerful God. Favor has found you.

Finances have found you. You are faithful and you know what to do. You shall do everything I have taught you, as the prophets are taught of Me.

The spirit of the Lord is upon you. You are My witnesses. Testimonies have been birthed right here on earth. All shall see where I brought you from, and the large place I have set you in.

You are shining in My divine. It's your time, so unwind. You have favor. Not just a moment, but a lifetime of favor that doesn't come with labor. Continue to walk out your wealth as you receive it all. **Health Overflow Wealth**. I shall continue to show you **HOW**. You shall continue to teach the people **HOW**.

I have released this wealth. All will see this is the Lord's doing, and it's marvelous in our sights. Continue to love Me with all your might. Your soul is anchored and your prosperity has come. I spoke this to My prophet, Apostle Leroy Thompson, and so are you prospering. Money just keeps on coming to you.

Money you didn't know was coming is here. I have made millions manifest to you. You have a new beginning without ending. You have a new look for a new life, without strife. You are walking in daily divine promotions. You have received My *Glorious Light*. You are living a *Great Lifestyle*. You are *Giving Love*. Your *Gifts* are *Leaping*.

March

MARCH 1, 2016

This is what Praise has done!

I never lose out on what God has brought about. Thy word have I hidden in my heart, oh God, and it shall never depart. Holy Spirit helps me to remember, retain, remain in every word and everything God has allowed, is allowing and shall continue to allow to come my way.

All my blessings are here to stay, because God brought them my way. I shall forever be grateful and thankful to God for all His benefits. I give thanks with a grateful heart. God is great and greatly to be praised.

Raise, raise, raise, because the price has been paid. Lift your hands and dance because God has blessed your finances.

Never give up. Never give in. God has already caused you to win. You shall never be bound in sin. God will always do it again, and again.

Never give up. Never give in. Again, God says, you always win. Know that God allowed His son to die for your sins; and He raised him up again. Always remember the cross experience.

In His crucification know that the price has already been paid: and for you He gave. You must never misbehave. Stay in obedience and love Me, your almighty, all powerful God. Do as I say, and promised blessings shall continue to come your way and stay. All I have belongs to you. You receive because you are My beloved ones. The victory has already been won, because of My beloved son.

Know you are here for this very reason. You were made in My image, modeled after Me. When people see you, they see Me. Never display what I haven't sent your way. You are joint heirs with My son.

What I have I give to you. Wealth and riches are in your house. I have brought them out: and given to you as an inheritance. Houses and land, it's all in My plan. I've given it all to man.

Many Mansions I've be stored and they are yours. I'm not a man. I never lie. Trust Me, rely on Me and this is how you multiply. Continue to pray, stay, and lay on your face before Me. I'm the one that has made you free. Free to soar to new levels. Free to have power over devils.

You are in the race because I set you there. Without Me you will never go there. There is the destination I allow you reach. Teach, tarry and triumph. This is your vision that's already been set for you.

Hear, listen and always do. I've made this all come to you. Believe and receive all the blessings from Me, your almighty, all-powerful God.

MARCH 6, 2016

Love Language

Live this life of love and laughter. God has given us a life of love that's spread abroad in our hearts, and it shall never depart, because He is never far. Always speak, and spread this Love Language. This is what God has commanded us to do, in this scripture.

> *Look! he said. The people are united, and they all speak the same language. After this, nothing they set out to do will be impossible for them!*
>
> Genesis 11:6 NLT.
>
> *We must also love God with all our hearts, as in this scripture.*
>
> *And you must love the LORD your God with all your heart, all your soul, all your mind, and all your strength.*
>
> Mark 12:30 NLT.

Now we have connected our Love Language and have love in our hearts: we must know that God has already set us apart. When we keep speaking, doing, and living in our Love Language God shall continue to daily load us with His benefits, which is in these scriptures.

> *He forgives all my sins and heals all my diseases. He redeems me from death and crowns me with love and tender mercies. He fills my life with good things. My youth is renewed like the eagle's! The LORD gives righteousness and justice to all who are treated unfairly.*
>
> Psalms 103:3-6 NLT.

Just like without faith it's impossible to please God: without love in our hearts it's impossible to keep receiving from God. I must continue to live, breathe, and receive from the Spirit of the Lord that's on me.

God has breathed the breath of life that's within us. Never fake and front with your love. God knows and shall reveal your Love Language. What's in your heart, that's what God will allow to come out.

You have won the victory, as God has fought the battle. Don't try and repay what God has already allowed his Son to pay for. God explains it better in the scripture:

> *Dearly beloved, avenge not yourselves, but rather give place unto wrath: for it is written, Vengeance is mine; I will repay, saith the Lord.*
>
> Romans 12:19 KJV

Keep speaking the same language, being that of your Love Language. God will continue to keep you from all hurt, harm, and danger. Pump up the volume. Never be silent. Shout, you are out!

The walls are down. God is always around. He never leaves or forsakes His own. The enemy has been smitten, for it is written; and satan has been kicked off his throne. Speak loud, spare not, God has given you all He's got.

Your Love Language is a seed, and God has already met the need. As God's children He shall continue to feed. You shall have what you say. Remember to always do everything God's way.

Speak the blessings and not the curse. You shall have what you speak into your purse. You shall eat what you speak. If you want apples, don't speak grapes. If you want supernatural unlimited supply of money to keep coming to you: don't speak what you see in front of you.

Trust that God already knows what He going to do. Now it's all up to you. I speak an abundant supply of prosperity. God has spoken it best in this scripture.

> *Beloved, I wish above all things that thou mayest prosper and be in health, even as thy soul prospereth.*
>
> 3 John 1:2 KJV

Speak God's Love Language and continue to do what He says to do, and all these blessings shall continue to come upon you and overtake you. In the beginning, God spoke it all into existence. Now you shall continue to speak everything to keep coming to you. I believe and I receive what's already been promised to me. I say yes and I agree to all God has and shall continue to give me.

MARCH 8, 2016

Never give voice to the enemy. Never let your thoughts override mine. I have delivered you right on time. You are walking in My divine. You shall continue to shine.

Let this mind be in you that's also in Christ Jesus. Never sit and sup in the wrong thoughts, they will rest in you. Step by step I have given you help. Holy Spirit beings this word from Me.

> *So shall they fear the name of the Lord from the west, and his glory from the rising of the sun. When the enemy shall come in like a flood, the Spirit of the Lord shall lift up a standard against him.*
>
> Isaiah 59:19 KJV

Go My way always. I have already made a way. My Blessings are here to stay and no one can take them away. Stay in your lane. My blood runs through your veins. Jesus, Jesus, Jesus, I have prepared you for this reason.

*1) **Kingdom Prosperity***

*2) **Kept Promises***

*3) **Kind People***

The kingdom is in need, that's why I have released prosperity. I have kept My promises. No cursed generation. Kind people, releasing, refreshing, resting in My promotions and provisions.

Favor, favor, favor and no labor. These people I have raised up to help you. Build My kingdom first; everything else has been given you. By Grace through faith you have received. Never cease to give Me the glory. Tell My story.

Testimonies I've given you. Do as I say to do. The blessings shall continue to come on you and overtake you. Prosperity is your birthright. I have released you tonight.

Thoughts that only come from Me. Think large. I'm never far. I've set you here. Think on these things. Power, riches, wisdom, strength, glory, honor, blessings. I'm not a man. I can't lie. I have created you to multiply, have dominion, subdue, replenish, I given you plenty. Believe, and receive, it's all from Me, your almighty, all-powerful God. Enjoy!!!

MARCH 10, 2016

1) Great Harvest
2) Giving Heart
3) Got Hope

You have *Great Harvest, Giving Heart, and you Got Hope.* Your time has come. You have won. The enemy's hands are concealed. You are healed of all manor of sickness and disease. What tried to break you has strengthened you. I used the thing that was a thorn in your flesh to *groom, grow, govern, and give* you abundance, and overflow.

The *Great Harvest* has come. Again, the enemy is defeated, for this very reason. This is your season. Never return or else you will burn. Ashes to ashes, dust to dust, your obedience is a must.

The seasons couldn't have come without the victory being won. It's all because of My son. You have this *Giving Heart* because you have been set apart. You *Got Hope* and you are no longer tied up in the rope. You are loosed into the harvest and out of the hooks of lack. There's no turning back. This is the large place of promises, promotions and prosperity that pleases me, your almighty, all-powerful God.

The kingdom of God is at hand. I have placed the money in your hands. Money is never an issue again. Whatever the price of the item you can pay. Nothing gets in your way. Don't look at the price and fear, just say bring it here. You are always in the driver's seat. Pull in the driveway; this is your place. Park. I've set you in this large place.

Enjoy, relax, rest, reign, you are in your lane. Believe, and receive; it's all from Me. Rejoice and be exceeding glad. I've given you the best life you ever had. No strings and no struggles attached.

Again, no lack. Your money is on track. Never look back. Full speed ahead.

Everywhere you look, sales have come in for your books. Many venues and plenty of revenue. Money is never a problem again. I shall continue to minister seed to you because you are a sower.

Give, live and forgive. Obey, stay and pray. Praise, prophesy and prosper. Laugh, leap and love this lifestyle. These are my commands that I commissioned, charge and chose for you.

Hear, listen and do as I have spoken to you: and the blessings shall always come on you and overtake you.

MARCH 10, 2016

CupBarer! What's In Your Cup?

Follow up with what's in your cup. Wisdom and word that's what's up. Overflow, overflow, overflow, that's how we roll. Your boats have docked. That's how we rock. The doors are open because God has knocked. Come in. Sit with us again.

I say to you Lord and Saviour of all the nations. Thank you God for giving us manifestations. As far as the east is from the west, these are avenues for God's very best. We have far more than the rest. We have passed many tests.

The lessons have been learned. These blessings we yearned and earned. We are spiritually discerned. Obedience and love is always the key. All these blessings are on me. Continue to pray in the spirit.

This is God's way of showing us how. How to do everything unto Him. How has it been done? By grace through faith. God shall continue to bring blessings our way.

Again, Follow up with what's in your cup. Live life more abundantly is in your cup. All sufficiency, and always abounding to every good work, it's in your cup. Work, work, work, that's what's up!

"I'm working a work in you, that's what I do."

"I complete the work: and that's not for you."

"Continue to dream, I'm in your seam."

The smallest place, people can't see, right now. I shall make manifest the full garments. The garments of worship and praise, that's what I've made. Praise and worship Me like never before. I'm responsible for all open doors. Walk in. Garments of *finances, faithfulness, and fruitfulness*. Garments of *healing, hope and harvest*. Garments of wisdom and wealth.

Multiply, multiply, multiply. I've given you supernatural surplus and supply. This is why. The kingdom of God is at hand. Stand, I've chosen to use man. You are girded up, geared up. These tools, you must use. My obedience, and love, never refuse. These are your lifeline. Cast the nets. Receive net-breaking blessings, all *designed, destined, and delivered* to you by way of My innumerable host of Angels. They are employed by you. They obey you. Let them do what they do, as I've commanded them to.

You determine your outcome. What you speak, make sure it's from Me. What you do, do all as unto Me. What you receive, make sure I have released. I have made it this way. It's all here to stay. Make sure you continue to do things My way.

I am, that I am, have spoken. I am the almighty, all-powerful, most high God. This is My Word, let it never depart: and you shall go far. Rejoice, and be exceedingly glad. Again I say rejoice.

MARCH 17, 2016

God's Love Day!

God is so good. I love Him with all my heart, mind, soul, and might. He's my everything. He's my rescue, refuge, redeemer and my strength.

I've got to tell all what He's done for me. He brought me out of darkness into His marvelous light. This light that shall continue to shine through me for Him so all the world can see what He's done for me.

This day I tell about a love that brought me through. God so loved me that He gave me the love of His life, His only begotten Son. I have won. I'm God's beloved one. God is worthy of all my praise. I celebrate. I worship Him in spirit, truth, and in strength.

I'm not the servant that went. I'm the one that was sent. I'm sent and set apart by God. I came to serve, as God deserves. I give Him the glory, as I tell my story. Where God has brought me from. Again, I have won because of His Son, Jesus the Christ, who saved my life. I'm forever grateful. I shall always be faithful.

All the glory belongs to God. I get no credit for this love of life. This life I live in love. I dance before the Lord as David did. I'm not ashamed of how I live. My worship and my praise is what God gave. This praise I couldn't have made. I shall praise Him all my days.

When you see me jumping and leaping; don't think I'm out of my mind. This is my time. God has allowed me to shine in His divine. When you see me talking and no one's there, when you see me crying and no one's there, just know someone is there but you can't see because the spirit of the Lord is upon me.

I testify and teach. I touch and reach. I talk and preach. I testify and teach what He's done and shall continue to do for me. I touch and reach who wants to be saved and changed. My talk and preach is the good news of the gospel that He's *instructed, impacted, and imparted* in me.

I teach, reach, and preach because of the kingdom of God that's within me. Souls shall continue to come because God's will is being done. Thank God for this, His Love Day. As blessings continue to come my way. In His will I shall always stay.

MARCH 18, 2016

Personal Word for me

All my company website visitors have become paying customers NOW!!!! All paying customers have come to me NOW. I have unlimited abundance and supernatural supply of paying customers coming to me. They buy and they multiply. I believe and I receive them NOW. I commission and I command my innumerable host of Angels to always bring all my paying customers to me. I believe and I receive them continually. Paying customers just keep on coming to me. Money just keeps on coming to me.

Our new home by Grand Homes original Hamptons Model desires for us to live in it NOW. We have received our favorable deal. On March 4, 2016 at the Houston SMC2U, Apostle Dr. Leroy Thompson said I was ready to receive as he proceeded to lay hands on me and imparted what God wanted me to receive. I have received, and the Spirit of the Lord is upon me. Everything Apostle Dr. Leroy Thompson has spoken to me according to God's Word and His will, I believe and I have received NOW.

I have the same grace on me as Apostle Dr. Leroy Thompson. Everything he owns, I own. I have come into my own, because of the seeds that I have sown. I have received all my blessings unknown. God is not a respecter of persons, what He's done for Apostle Dr. Leroy Thompson he has done the same in principle for me. I walk in the same Spiritual anointing as he does. Holy Spirit takes over in my life as he does in his life. I behold my blessings as they unfold.

I declare that I am a God-made miracle millionaire. It's not a mistake. I am set in this large place, for Christ's sake. I teach, I preach, and I reach, for the kingdom's sake.

Our marriage, our money, and our ministries are manifesting NOW. We are *flooding, flowing, and flourishing, in finances by grace through faith.* God has already sent the blessings our way. We have received. UPE Designs, GNLD, and *T.S.I.T.S. Things Seen In The Spirit* have caused wealth and riches to be in my house, never to be evicted out.

"This wealth came quickly, sudden, and right now," says the almighty, all-powerful God. I have received all the blessings that have been given me. People will see this is the Lord's doing and it's marvelous in our sights. We shall continue to love the Lord thy God with all our hearts, and with all our soul, and with all our might: as we live right.

MARCH 22, 2016
Know These Four Words From God

1) Confirming
2) Convicting
3) Compassionate
4) Continuing

God always sends a *Confirming* word, that's *Convicting*, *Compassionate*, and *Continuing* to help build up the body of Christ. This is the word that came through the dream God gave me on March 22, 2016. Take heed. Hear this.

When the storms come, you must not be afraid. Look the storm in the eye; take a picture of it, and quickly it goes bye-bye. God hasn't given us the spirit of fear, he's given us power, love and a sound mind. This is why He says this in His Word.

> *Then saith Jesus unto him, Get thee hence, Satan: for it is written, Thou shalt worship the Lord thy God, and him only shalt thou serve. Then the devil leaveth him, and, behold, angels came and ministered unto him.*
>
> Matthew 4:10-11 KJV

> *When the enemy comes as we know he will, we must not give in to his schemes. God reminds us that he has no means. His word says this. So that Satan will not outsmart us. For we are familiar with his evil schemes.*
>
> 2 Corinthians 2:11 NLT

God has already given us power over Devils. We have been placed and positioned at another level. We never accept anything less ever again. We have been given our **VIP** status from God Himself.

1) **V**ictories
2) **I**ncrease
3) **P**rosperity

Never accept what people say you are, know that God says you are Supernaturally Supplied. Your fruit always multiplies. Everything God creates grows. How? I don't know. My part is doing it all as unto Him. I never sit idly by and wait for the bye and bye. God is my source, sustainer, and trainer.

I know what to do and when to do. I go where He says to go. I go into the world compelling and telling the souls to come into the kingdom of God, where there's *rest, rescue, reign, redemption, restoration,* for your soul.

Receive all from God He's the one that has provided blessings untold. Behold, see what God has done. He's given victory all because of His Son. We have won.

By grace through faith, continue to follow God's way. We understand that there is a way that seems right to man, but that's not in God's plan. Believe you have received all your blessings that came from Me. I am the almighty, all-powerful God that has spoken. Enjoy!!!

MARCH 29, 2016

Get GCW going again. Keep flowing, even in the not knowing. You are still growing. Stay in place. Don't get out of the race. You are not off beat. I put the running in your feet. Continue running.

I have given you plenty money. You are living in this land that flows with milk and honey. This land of no scarceness. No lack. You are on track. You breeze through every attack. Everything the enemy has stolen, I have given it back.

Victories, victories, victories, and vindication, I have set you before nations. People will hear and see, all that only comes from Me.

The rhythm is in the running of the race; make sure you keep up the pace. You will never fall on your face. All is done for Christ's sake. I make no mistake. I have sealed up the holes with blessings untold.

Every stone that was thrown I have used to build your home. This home that's built on a solid foundation, again, I have set you before nations. Speak My word. Men, women, boys, and girls, you shall be heard.

Pray the prayer of prophecy. Speak My word. TLC. Throw the Line and Catch. Reel in the ones that grab ahold, the ones that don't, let them go.

No stress, struggle, or strain, you are in My vein. Never complain. Just do it all in My name. Your life will never be the same.

Your family and friends that are faithfully connected to Me are connected to you. The doors are opened and doors are closed. The doors that were closed, I now open. The doors that were opened not by Me, I now close.

Enter into My place of peace, promises, provisions, promotions, and prosperity. Know that I have done this for you. Why? My kingdom is at hand, and I need someone willing to stand. Follow My plans. Continue to stand. Keep worshipping Me in spirit and in truth, and watch Me continue to make it happen for you.

Praise me without hesitation, always from the heart. Loving me is key to all that keeps coming from Me. People will see how you love Me, and how I cause you to love them. Continue to pray, stay, and do it My way. Pray for those who have gone astray and those whom I have told to stay. Pray for those who are doing things My way.

I have prepared the people to assist with the tasks. They are waiting for the word I have sent through you by way of Holy Spirit. Step out. You have people waiting to help bring it about. Have no doubt. It's all been worked out.

Money is never a problem. Money shall keep coming, as people will keep growing, and sowing. People will obey and release the money I have allowed to come their way. Money is here to stay.

In your going out and your coming in, I'm blowing them in like a mighty rushing wind. Quickly, suddenly. The white fields are already harvested. The harvest is plenteous, but the laborers are few, just remember to keep doing what I say to do.

There's no time for running in place, pick up the pace. It's all done for Christ's sake. He paid the price, the ultimate sacrifice. Now it's pay back time. Walk in His divine as if your life is on the line. This is the word from your almighty, all-powerful, loving, unchanging God!

April

APRIL 5, 2016

J.I.G.S.A.W.

Just
Increase
Giving
Supernatural
Abundance
Wealth

Just increase giving, supernatural abundance and wealth will come. Stand still and know that I'm God. See My Word in this scripture:

> *But you will not even need to fight. Take your positions; then stand still and watch the LORD's victory. He is with you, O people of Judah and Jerusalem. Do not be afraid or discouraged. Go out against them tomorrow, for the LORD is with you!*
>
> 2 Chronicles 20:17 NLT

I'm here. I'm always near. I never leave or forsake you. Continue to stay, pray and say. I have given you a voice. Hear, listen and do everything as unto Me. You have My Word that never returns void, it accomplishes what I please and prospers where I send it.

The spirit of the Lord is upon you. You shall teach, reach and preach the gospel. The acceptable year of our Lord and Savior. The power of God is resting upon you. Again, just do what I say to do. Don't worry. Don't fret. I have taken care of the rest. You are My very elect. My best. You excel far above the rest. You have passed test after test. You are set. You have received the lessons in the testing.

The testimonies must come forth. Never be ashamed or afraid to say what I've done for you. I've brought you through. When people think you are in the dark, just remember light is always revealed through darkness. Just like in the beginning, this world was dark, empty and without form. I brought light, filled the earth and shaped it. See this scripture:

> *In the beginning God created the heavens and the earth. The earth was formless and empty, and darkness covered the deep waters. And the Spirit of God was hovering over the surface of the waters. Then God said, "Let there be light," and there was light. And God saw that the light was good. Then he separated the light from the darkness.*
>
> Genesis 1:1-4 NLT

Be ye also ready. You shall go into the highways and byways and compel them to come. Victories after victories you have won, all because of My Son. The light and lamp is on. People will see and say I sent you. They will tell you, I sent them to help you. This has already been happening. Remember you never meet a stranger; they are the Angels that I made you aware of. See this scripture:

> *Don't forget to show hospitality to strangers, for some who have done this have entertained angels without realizing it!*
>
> Hebrews 13:2 NLT

> *Innumerable angels are Ascending and descending. See this scripture:*
>
> *No, you have come to Mount Zion, to the city of the living God, the heavenly Jerusalem, and to countless thousands of angels in a joyful gathering.*
>
> Hebrews 12:22 NLT

You will never want for anything. You have My word on it. I'm not a man. I can't lie. I place you here to bare fruit; they remain, multiply, and have dominion, never give your opinion. Again, the spirit of the Lord is upon you. The captives are set free when you follow Me. It's never about you; it's what I speak through you, by way of My Holy Spirit. See this scripture:

> *The Spirit of the LORD is upon me, for he has anointed me to bring Good News to the poor. He has sent me to proclaim that captives will be released, that the blind will see, that the oppressed will be set free, and that the time of the LORD's favor has come.*
>
> Luke 4:18-19 NLT

I've chosen you. You didn't choose you. You must speak the same language in all that you do. See My Word in these scriptures:

> *"You didn't choose me. I chose you. I appointed you to go and produce lasting fruit, so that the Father will give you whatever you ask for, using my name."*
>
> John 15:16 NLT

> *Look!" he said. "The people are united, and they all speak the same language. After this, nothing they set out to do will be impossible for them!*
>
> Genesis 11:6 NLT

You have made and shall continue to make tracks in the spirit. The people have a path to follow. I've set you up for such a time as this. People will say show me **HOW.** *Health Overflow Wealth.* I have given men for the vision and people to help support the kingdom and your life. *Prayer, praise, prophesy, and preach. All of these please Me and you receive your prosperity.*

APRIL 6, 2016

When you have no launch, you have no reach, you have no leap, and you can't launch out into the deep. When you don't do what God called you to do, you will lose sight of the destination where God wants to take you. Never cease to walk in your path that God has set you on. The straight and narrow path that all will not walk in. They are designed for you to win.

Never be a slave to sin. You are in control. Don't stay in it because you think people don't know.

I'm your all-knowing, everywhere, ever-present God. I chastise those who are My beloved and receive chastising. I let go of those who refuse the blood, and want to please the flesh. You must love Me with all your heart, body, soul, mind and might.

Just because I give you words to teach doesn't mean you are in My reach. I use whom I please for the kingdom's sake. I make no mistake. I bless you for the kingdom's sake. You will not be fulfilled being out of My will.

You will always be just taking a ride and never driving because of your hidden agenda. You must decide to drive at all times, or else you will always be just taking a ride.

Remember I know who's behind the wheel, of everything you are in, outside of My will, and when you think no one can see the driver (satan). You can't get in and out of the car with satan, you will never make it to your destination. You will always be just taking a ride letting him drive. It's time to keep the wheel always and not just walk in My will sometimes.

I'm a jealous God. When you put the flesh before Me, My wrath is placed upon you. This I do because I love you and want you to change. You must do it all in Jesus' name.

Sin has satan's blood. You have My blood. Ask yourself before you please the flesh: Is there any blood on it? My Son's death and resurrection was not in vain. Again I say, do it all in Jesus' name. The name above all names.

When sin and flesh call your name, refuse to answer. Hear Me. Don't shut Me out. I'm your almighty, all-powerful God. Your ears must be tuned to My voice, as My ears are tuned to your voice. I need you and you need Me. We can't work alone. You are My very elect, that I own. What you hear and see I let it be known.

Receive of Me all the time. Make up your mind. You must walk with Me all the time. Choose life and not death. Choose the blessings and not the curses. You can't keep going behind the curtain thinking it will never be opened. It will be opened and you will be exposed to the light.

I speak to those of you who want to walk in light and never worry about trying to stay hidden behind the curtain thinking you won't be exposed to light. All curtains will be drawn at some point in time. Stay out from behind the curtain. Let your light shine.

Walk in My divine at all times. This is My will for you. Hear, listen, and do. I'm pleased to prosper you. Receive from Me your almighty, all-powerful God!

APRIL 13, 2016

RoundUp Pesticide

This pesticide is used to kill everything that stops your vegetation. Nothing shall stop your crops from growing. Keep sowing. The seeds are planted and the harvest has come. I give you this chemical that's made by man. I've placed the blessings in your hands. This chemical is made to destroy everything that could stop or block what I've already made to manifest.

There are no side effects to My blessings. It's all good. Just love, obey, and serve. This chemical doesn't affect the nerves: It's vital to your blood flow that runs through your veins.

My blessings that I have given remain. Relax. Sit back. You shall never have any lack. You have made the tracks. My people have the living examples. The enemy will never deplete or defeat you. You have been elevated to higher levels. Never worry or be afraid of next level devils. I have chosen you for the tasks.

Never cover up or hide what I've provided. All shall see what I've done for thee. You are in line. It's My divine. Follow the instructions carefully. Never deviate from them. Your destination depends on these directions. Follow through. I've made it all happen for you.

What looks like a roadblock isn't an indication to stop. Remember Round Up Pesticide has already been applied. Your vegetation shall be seen by the nations. People will see what white fields of harvest I've already provided for thee. They have seen what lack and not enough look like.

Continue to serve and love Me with all your soul and might. This is key. Obey and serve. You will always spend your days in prosperity and your years in pleasure. Blessings that you can't measure. Unlimited.

Supernatural abundance. Harvest time is here. Never ending. Your sowing is growing. Continue sowing. Crops have come from everywhere. Even from seeds you didn't put or plant there. The soil is rich. Round Up has removed all the weeds. Nothing stops your seeds. Never forget that it was and shall always be Me that made it happen for thee. I am the almighty all-powerful God.

APRIL 14, 2016

Dig it! Dump it!

Dig up the ground!
Dump it in the grave!

Everything that we allowed to come alive should have stayed buried. Never bring it up again. You won't win. The enemy wants to bring up and remind you of all past hurt and pain. God says it shall not remain. Jesus didn't die in vain for you to still be in pain. All your heart aches and headaches must leave today. After all, you are the one that made it this way. God says release them now they can't stay.

The dirt has been turned and tossed. Just like your wrong mindset. All your needs have been met. Just because you haven't seen the manifestation yet, doesn't mean it hasn't been released. God has laid it all at your feet. He says remember Me when you come into your kingdom. Never cease to pray and praise God. Never let your mind take you places you can't recover from. There's no need to think anything other than what God has preserved and promised you.

Always stay in the position and place of rest and receiving. God promotes and prosperity regardless of what you see. God has allowed you to see what you say. All these blessings have come your way. They are here to stay. You must get out of the way. Allow God to help move the dirt and dig it and dump it. **Dig up the ground and dump it in the grave.** All the things you made.

God is ready to do a new thing with you. It's time to see what you say. Receive all today. Look, like, and love life. Rejoice and be exceedingly glad. You have more money than you ever had. The millions have manifested. Receive your supernatural blessings.

Those temporary light afflictions have been dumped. Cover the grave because the price has been paid. Foundations have been laid. Follow through on what God has told you to do. There's nothing He will withhold from you.

You must continue in His lane. Never remain the same. God has sent the rain. Resources will never be a problem, because The Source has released the supernatural surplus. God is your source, supplier, sustainer and He's all-sufficient.

Stretch out your rod. The Red Sea is open. Walk through. All this land is for you. Enjoy. Never dig up what God allowed to be buried.

Blessings have come in a hurry. Never worry. You are out of the grave of lack. No turning back. This time has been coming. You have been waiting, praying, praising and staying before Me, your almighty, all-powerful God. I have taken you far. Higher levels, living, and learning. This is My pleasure. Receive and Rejoice!!!

APRIL 20, 2016

#Wisdom
#WisDomion

These allow you to replenish, subdue, multiply and receive all the blessings that have been set up for you. Praise, praise, praise is what God says.

Pray, praise, prophesy and preach without ceasing. Never stop what I've started in you. This is what I've chosen you to do.

Teach and reach the Unreachable! The ones you know of and don't know of. You have been *chosen, conditioned, charged, convinced, and confirmed* for the task. The enemy has shot his biggest bullets, but they couldn't kill you. You were wounded and the weapons were formed, but they could never prosper.

Stay in My lane. This is the straight and narrow path that I've opened up for you. Continue to do what I've said to do. The way, wisdom, word and wealth have been given to you. Obey and serve, this is what you deserve. My righteousness remaineth forever.

Wise Dominion is your birthright. You are hearing, listening and doing what I've said to do. Never let anyone or anything stop you. Continue in My direction and you will see your destination. More places to go and gain and remain in Me. You have been in the presence of My best.

Being in the presence and atmosphere at the visionary conference of Jesse Duplantis was a big part of your destination. **The laying on of hands and receiving the transference of the wealth and anointing is on you.** You have received the blessings from Me. Never be deceived. People will see and listen to you because of the interview at this conference. I've given you favor without labor. Receive. I've set you in places to be seen and heard from the nations. I never change My mind.

You shall indeed shine and walk in My divine. You will never be behind. You are a leader. I called you because of your love and willingness to work for Me. No distraction or devastation can destroy you.

You've been through the worst in your marriage, ministry and even money. I've given you the greatest marriage, ministry, and yes, money shall keep on coming to you. In all you do, continue to keep praying, praising, preaching, and prophesying. You do your part and I will do Mine. We are in this harvest field together. We need each other.

Keep Wisdom and work it, it will work for you. Wise Dominion is yours forever. Receive, receive, and always receive. This is your **HOW!** *Heath Overflow Wealth.* Even when you don't know HOW! Keep moving. Don't stop. You are out. You are My kingdom supporter. That's why you have received

Wise Dominion. You shall know what to do, because I shall continue to show you.

The gates are open. The nations are open to hear you. Even when you don't know how right now. This is the wealth you shall continue to flow and flourish in, supernatural abundantly, and unlimited supply. Receive dominion. Replenish, subdue, and multiply.

APRIL 26, 2016

Commentary

A systematic series of explanations and interpretations (as of a writing)

God has made me a commentary for Him. I shall speak the words spoken from Him to me by way of Holy Spirit. I shall continue to pray the prayer of prophecy. I'm convinced and confident with what God has spoken and allowed to come.

I decree and declare everything that God speaks to me and through me for His people. I confront everything contrary to the will of God for His people. I shall give explanations of what God has said and is saying, in this present time, and times to come.

God's glory is revealed through us from His presence and our experiences. People will be drawn to God from these life experiences spoken and shown by us, of what God has done through us by His spirit. Revelations are revealed, and released.

Through **SPAH**, I'm raised up for these times and seasons of favor by grace through faith, because God has made it this way. This is **SPAH**, the *Suffering Prophetic Anointing* and *Healing* from God. The world will hear instructions, and information divinely directed, and delivered to His people: which will bring inspiration, interpretation, and impartation from God. In my suffering its for Christ's sake and not my own. His word explains it here.

> *For God called you to do good, even if it means suffering, just as Christ suffered for you. He is your example, and you must follow in his steps."*
>
> 1 Peter 2:21 NLT

> *For examples of patience in suffering, dear brothers and sisters, look at the prophets who spoke in the name of the Lord.*
>
> James 5:10 NLT

I the Lord called you and appointed and anointed you for the tasks ahead: even before you or anyone knew you.

> *I knew you before I formed you in your mother's womb. Before you were born I set you apart and appointed you as my prophet to the nations.*
>
> Jeremiah 1:5 NLT

I shall lay hands on the sick and the sick be healed. I shall decree a thing and it shall be established unto thee. I shall call healing and it comes, immediately. Because of your healing in the areas of your marriage, mind, ministry and money you are ready for the journey.

APRIL 26, 2016

December 31, 2015 God spoke for the year 2016

2016 The Year We Receive Everything

> *Beloved, I wish above all things that thou mayest prosper and be in health, even as thy soul prospereth.*
>
> 3 John 1:2 KJV

The three most important things we will receive in this year is:

1) Optimum of Health
2) Overflow of Harvest
3) Outpouring of Holy Spirit

First we must know these key points:

1) *In the beginning God created the heaven and the earth.* Genesis 1:1 KJV

2) *For God so loved the world, that he gave his only begotten Son, that whosoever believeth in him should not perish, but have everlasting life.* John 3:16 KJV

3) *In the beginning was the Word, and the Word was with God, and the Word was God.* John 1:1 KJV

The five most important keys on how to receive these three things are:
    1) Seeking the Savior Matthew 6:33
    2) Sowing the Seeds John 3:16
    3) Studying the Scriptures 2 Timothy 2:15
    4) Submitting to Holy Spirit Acts 1:8
    5) Speaking what God Says Numbers 23:12

We must be Grateful to God for these three things
    1) Rising of Son
    2) Remission of Sins
    3) Receiving of Supernatural

We must remember that God is the creator of all things; He loves us so that He gave His only precious Son, who is the love of His life. We must model after Him, which is loving and giving.

Know that God gave the Word which was made flesh. The Word of God is His being and the Word is with Him and shall continue to be who He is.

Our minds must be in line with our mouths. We must think before we speak. Be mindful of what we say. Model after what God does. Have God on our minds as He has us on His mind. The scripture says:

> *The Lord hath been mindful of us: he will bless us; he will bless the house of Israel; he will bless the house of Aaron.*
>
> Psalms 115:12 KJV

Holy Spirit must always be present in our minds, so we can think the thoughts that God has given, is giving, and shall continue to give us. This is a year we will receive like never before from God by way of Holy Spirit. Stay tuned in. Turn up. Make sure you hear God's voice and not the enemy. His voice overrides the enemy, however you must be tuned into the right channel.

You shall receive brand new revelations daily. Never miss what He's speaking because you don't know your time of exit. Be watchful, waiting to hear, listen and do. God has an awesome work for you. Be ye also ready as the Word says,

> *Understand this: If a homeowner knew exactly when a burglar was coming, he would not permit his house to be broken into. You also must be ready all the time, for the Son of Man will come when least expected.*
>
> Luke 12:39-40 NLT

You have been chosen to receive the secrets that God wants the world and the body of Christ to know. He reveals to the believers who want to and are willing to walk and worship Him in spirit and in truth. Seek Him first and foremost, and everything shall be added unto you in this year of 2016.

The kingdom of God is at hand; it's already been placed in your hands. Continue your assignment, which is to walk, work, and be willing to always *demonstrate, display, dominate, demand, decree,* and do everything God has chosen, commanded and commissioned you for.

You are on the mantels displaying and demonstrating your dominion. You have an awesome *marriage, and ministry, that's manifesting along with money that's mounted, motivated and moving in your hands Now!* Live in righteousness. Receive revelations. Render service.

The spirit of the Lord has set up residence in your heart and never to be evicted or moved out. Shout, shout, shout. Holy Spirit brings it all about.

APRIL 26, 2016

The enemy has to seek who is willing to let him in. Stay hidden under the wings of the almighty God, in the secret place of His pavilion or tabernacle. God is my rock, my fortress, my hiding place, therefore the enemy can't touch me as long as I don't reveal myself to him.

Demons will test you, like they tested Jesus. You are made in his image. So is Jesus, so are you. You must stand and stay strong. No bowing and bending to the enemy. If you are not with Jesus, you are against him, and working against him.

We must work and walk this world together being in Christ Jesus. Make sure we are always *remembering, recognizing, realizing, remaining, resting, reigning, ruling, and receiving from the Cross of Christ's experience.* We are dead to sin and alive in Christ Jesus. We must cast out and keep out all demonic forces that try to keep us in bondage.

We are risen with Christ and we seek those things which are above, where Christ is seated on the right side of God. *Stay seated, suited, surrounded, and spiritually sound in the supernatural things of God, in Christ Jesus.*

You will have shut down all the tricks and schemes of satan and his devices. Know that God has given you your weapons. Use them. See what they are in this scripture.

> A final word: *Be strong in the Lord and in his mighty power. Put on all of God's armor so that you will be able to stand firm against all strategies of the devil. For we are not fighting against flesh-and-blood enemies, but against evil rulers and authorities of the unseen world, against mighty powers in this dark world, and against evil spirits in the heavenly places. Therefore, put on every piece of God's armor so you will be able to resist the enemy in the time of evil. Then after the battle you will still be standing firm. Stand your ground, putting on the belt of truth and the body armor of God's righteousness. For shoes, put on the peace that comes from the Good News so that you will be fully prepared. In addition to all of these, hold up the shield of faith to stop the fiery arrows of the devil. Put on salvation*

as your helmet, and take the sword of the Spirit, which is the word of God. Pray in the Spirit at all times and on every occasion. Stay alert and be persistent in your prayers for all believers everywhere. And pray for me, too. Ask God to give me the right words so I can boldly explain God's mysterious plan that the Good News is for Jews and Gentiles alike. I am in chains now, still preaching this message as God's ambassador. So pray that I will keep on speaking boldly for him, as I should.

Ephesians 6:10-20 NLT

May

MAY 4, 2016

Connections are Important

Who are you connected to, and allowing to speak to you? We are first connected to God and all that's connected to Him, His son Jesus, Holy Spirit, and His angels. We are connected to our spouses, children, relatives, and then the kingdom of God.

When we are connected together as husband and wife, there should be agreement. How shall two walk together, except in agreement? When two shall agree as touching, God will do everything for you.

In marriage we are to cleave to each other and leave father and mother. Be connected to each other first in love, then you can spread love everywhere else. No connection at home will cause disconnection at home and everywhere else. God honors connections.

We must be on one accord, speak the same language and there's nothing we could ever imagine that He won't do for us. No one else can fit in our marriage connection. They weren't designed to fit. Let no one get in between and disconnect. We are fitly joined together. Every misconnect is designed to disconnect. Don't try and connect with those that God hasn't put together. What God put together no one can separate.

Never say this is for God's sake when you doing it for your sake. If it doesn't fit, never force it, for if you do it will soon be broken. If you leave an opening, the enemy will come in and try to make you sin.

Again, connections are important. Stay connected to the people and things of God, and you will always go far. If you disconnect, Gods promises you will never get. Rejoice and receive!

MAY 10, 2016

1) Supernatural Sound
2) Sovereign Saviour
3) Sinners Saved
4) Sufficient Supply

Hear the voice of the Lord. He's given us the *Supernatural Sound* from heaven. He's our *Sovereign Saviour. Sinners are Saved.* We have *Sufficient Supply* and our fruits multiply. Your new life has begun because of what you have done. You have prayed, stayed, and forgave. You shall receive blessings now and always.

Continue to press, push, pull and be in position. You are on a mission. Many people shall come your way, however they will not stay. More will be many as I allow plenty. This new life I've divinely designed for you, to keep moving regardless of what people do.

Your good days shall always outweigh the bad days. See happiness even in your sadness. Keep *praying, pressing, pushing and pulling*. The harvest is plentiful but the laborers are few. I've chosen you and showed you what to do. Holy Spirit shall continue to be with, and help you.

Call, command, confess, commit, and be confident in everything I've commissioned you to do. Never be afraid. I'm with you always. You have My ear. I've heard your cry and call. Keep hold of My hand, stand, and you shall never fall.

The wait is over. It's your time, to shine in My divine. You are off the sideline. The race never ended. I had to pull you out until I finished. Things came that made you drop. That's why I made you stop. I've pulled and picked you up, because you said enough is enough, as things continued to get rough.

You are tough. Keep it moving, because I've made you built to last. There was shaking in the storm, but never breaking. You came through because My hand is always on you.

Speak to the world. Tell your testimony. Thousands shall come because of what I've done. The kingdom is at hand, again stand.

You will always hear the Supernatural Sound of the Sovereign Saviour, as I've blessed you with favor and no labor. Steps are made, and Sinners are Saved, because of the steps you have made and paved the way.

There's hope, healing, harvest and wholeness, because of your boldness. Receive My **Sufficient Supply.** Again you are built to last, and never bound by your past. Again you have prayed, stayed, and forgave, continue doing things My way. I'm the one and only, your all-powerful, almighty God. Be happy, and exceedingly glad. Enjoy this great life you never had.

MAY 16, 2016

Cruising the oceans for our 17th Year Anniversary on the 15th

As I travel, I see what I see, all these promises that God has given me. I receive always, blessings that God has allowed to come upon me and overtaken me. My eyes are open, in the ocean. Motion after motion, I've received my portion. From port to port, anchors are weighed, because the price was paid.

As I sit, I remember and recall, Jesus paid it all. I receive. God's anointing I carry. The vision tarries. I Wait. The vision has been written. It's plain, personal, and portable. It's speaking, never lying. Though people are dying, I'm flying. Soaring to higher heights. I have kept the faith, and I never gave up in the fight. I love You with all my might.

Special events I shall present. Everything I've spoken I meant. Hear Me, I am the Lord God. I am speaking to you, revealing what I want from you and what I want you to do. Do as I say to do. I shall always provide for you. You are My chosen generation.

Again, you shall speak to the nations. Thousands and thousands shall fall, but nothing shall come near your dwelling places. As I put down one, I pick up another. What I've done for one, I've done for others.

You are My beloved. I've blessed your going out and your coming in. I've allowed you to win. I've given you everything. This is My pleasure.

Prosperity is your birthright. What you were born with is your inheritance. You are joint heirs with My Son, Jesus Christ. Remember to always live right. The prayers of the righteous availeth much. Now, live as such.

People recognize the anointing on you. They do as I tell them to do for you. Don't be surprised when strangers recognize you. They stop and talk because of your walk. They desire to be in your presence because of My pleasure.

Be careful of entertaining strangers, they are My angels, of that you shall beware. I've sent them there. Each one has his purpose. You shall give them what they need, and receive what they give you from Me. Don't think it's strange; receive in Jesus' name. Never discredit, or despise the small things, it's all from Me.

You've been given your supernatural supply. Receive, and multiply. Everything I give grows, even things you don't know, Holy Spirit reveals what I give. You are never in the dark. Shine in My divine.

Keep sailing. Never failing. Many destinations, I'm sending you to. It's all set up for you.

This is the year of plenty. I'm sending many. People will come to your ministry. This ministry I've set you in to win. Souls will come from near and far. I've set the bar. No limits.

Kingdom reign, because of My name and the name of Jesus. Receive in this season. Living waters, you are traveling. Many waters you are traveling. These waters are for you to see and supersede, far greater than the rest.

The test has been passed. Never repeat it. This week you will receive your favor, without labor. Seven days of completion. The eighth day is your birthday. The new beginning of dominion. Expect the great.

I've allowed this all to come your way. Never stop praising Me and giving Higher praise. Your Worship has raised. You shall give and receive in your new family connection. These are your blessings.

Your new church location I'm sending you is through your new family connection. Your new home, you now own. You been confessing, and calling, it's yours for the asking. Revisit, receive. It's waiting for you.

Don't be afraid of the price. You don't know how or where the money will come, know that I've already supernaturally provided. The birds eat the worms from the dirt on earth. I provide their food. I cause people to throw food on the ground for them. The how you don't know right now. Just do your part. I've done mine.

Listen carefully to My spirit. You will never miss it. Move when I say move, don't try to figure it out. Go even when it looks like nothing, even when you can't see. When you look out at night sailing the ocean, in the night hours you see nothing, but you know your ship is still sailing. You don't stop sailing. Keep following the compass. It knows the direction that's been set.

Know the direction that I've set. I am the almighty, all-powerful God that made this all happen. Receive. It's your time indeed. Rejoice and be exceedingly glad!

MAY 17, 2016

Shake, shake, shake, God has caused an earthquake. God is shaking up things right here on Earth. Be ready. Keep it steady. Keep the faith. He makes no mistake. Continue to do things His way. He has moved mountains. You draw from the fountain. Rivers are flowing. Again, God is showing. The four winds are blowing.

Bless the Lord oh my soul, and all that is within me. Tarry, wait, God has made the way. It's all about the kingdom's sake. Walls are down. God is always around. Angels are delivering, and dumping your dominion. This is just the beginning. Your time has come.

You're not just winning, you have won. Shout, shout, shout, God has given you the house. Never doubt, God has brought you out. Out of debt and into wealth. Out of stress and into great health. Stride, strut your stuff. Never make excuses for your wealth.

People will be amazed, some will be confused, you're the one God chose to use. Look at what God has done, it's marvelous in our sight. Continue to love God with all your might. Live right. Continue to write. You have the vision; it's plain and shall remain.

There maybe some tests, trials, and temptations, however you shall reach the nations. God called you for this very reason. It's your season. They never cease. Increase, increase, increase.

God has done it for me. I'm soaring in the unknowing, because of the all knowing, all-powerful, all-sufficient God. I'm working in the kingdom. I'm drinking, never draining, or in drought. I open my mouth, and I speak it out. God is wonderful. He's willing, and waiting for you to receive His wealth.

Step, step, step, you have help. Holy Spirit is in you. He's pouring, pushing, positioning, and placing you in the promises of prosperity.

Receive. You have no need. You shall always supersede. You have crossed the line. The finish is on. You won, because of God's Son. Enjoy the victories.

MAY 20, 2016

No pain can remain in Jesus' name. No sickness or disease can remain in me and take me over. I'm blessed, healed, delivered and set free from everything that tries to take me over. I got the power, and I use my power to cast out all demonic forces of the enemy now, in Jesus' name.

I believe and I receive everything that God has promised, has given, and shall continue to give me. Nothing and no one can stop, or take away, what God allows to come my way. I'm supernaturally, abundantly supplied. Everything God gave and continues to give me is multiplied. So is Jesus so I'm I.

As Jesus' blood flows through my veins, my power and my fruit remains. In Jesus' name. Nothing can hold me down. Nothing can hold me back. I have no lack and no limits. God has given me plenty. Sickness and disease, I don't have any. Nothing can harm, hurt, hinder, or hold me down, because God is always around. He's never far. He's forever in my heart. My heart is true, and God says "I can trust you."

Faithful, that's my stand. Living righteous is always the plan. I hold fast, and I know that God's promises, provisions, promotions, and prosperity last. I will never be stuck, stagnated, and stopped because of my past. I have pressed, and pushed from pain to pleasure.

Prosperity I receive. This gives God pleasure to prosper me. I enjoy the finer things in life. I love God with all my heart, mind, soul and might. I continue to live right.

MAY 21, 2016
Restoration Rejuvenation Render Receive

You have been *restored, rejuvenated, rendered service, and receive* everything I've set in motion for you. Again, you shall speak to the nations. Keep your place. Do it My way. Your way might look good to you, but do what I say to do. You can never go wrong.

Look out. I've given you this shout. Again, don't go back to the sin you were in. You will never win. Just because you think you are hiding from people, you can never hide from Me, I see.

Your mind is your time with Me. Think on the thoughts I give you. Do what I say to do. I shall always provide for you. Don't look back. You are on track. You have no lack. No limitation.

Again, you shall reach the nations. Just because you see negative, doesn't mean it's not positive. This light affliction is only for a moment. Don't get stuck in the moment. Keep pushing and pressing. I've made you a blessing, to be blessed. You are My very best. I chose, commissioned, and commanded you to go.

Even when you don't know where you're going, just remember to go because I said so and sent you there. Where is revealed in the how. Allow My Holy Spirit to speak to you now.

Signs and wonders shall follow those that believe. In the days to come you will see. Sit tight. Do things right and I will allow you to see where I want you to be.

Keep meditating on the scriptures. Praying in the spirit. All things shall be revealed. Quickly, suddenly, right now. You will not see if you go back to where I delivered you from. This is not a game. You will not win or see where I want you to be if you don't follow Me. When you get there, don't think you can go back.

These are the most important days of your marriage, ministry, and money. Don't stop mediating, praying, and speaking My scriptures, which is the Word I've given to you. Love Me with all your heart, mind, body, soul, and might. The questions you shall be asked are for a reason. Don't think it's strange, they are in My name. I will give you what to say.

Keep your ears and eyes on Me. Yes. I've given this all to you, for such a time as this. The people are looking, searching for answers. I've given the answers to you. Make sure you speak what I told you to.

Your marriage is key to all that you will receive from Me. You must not have hidden agendas. Again, remember you will not receive, if you don't shut down completely what I allowed you to be delivered from, and have forgiven you for. Shut the door. I will not say it any more.

Receive. Receive. Receive. The blessings that are in motion to thee. It's My pleasure to prosper you.

MAY 26, 2016

R.I.P.	**I**
Released	Take
Increase	**IT**
Prosperity	

RIP. The world calls it **Rest In Peace**. **RIP**. In the kingdom, God calls it **Released Increase Prosperity**. We have to say **I Take** IT to our prosperity.

Don't stand around waiting and wondering and asking, Is this for me? God wants us to prosper in our souls as well as health. Take our health and wealth. Receive it. Live healthy, whole lives, full of hope and harvest.

We can't possess that which we don't go get. God says the wealth and riches are in our houses. It's already been provided by grace through faith. I Reach out and receive what God has given me.

We must be strong in the Lord and in the power of His might. Live right. The price has been paid. Steps have been made. You've made tracks in the spirit that can't be erased. Everything we've asked according to His will has been granted. Follow the leadership of Holy Spirit; not your spirit. God's Spirit will never lead or guide you in the wrong direction.

Always be ready to make corrections. Never leave your connections. The trail shall never be cold, because of what you know. Every place the soles of your feet tread upon is yours. It's according to God's will.

Never go by what you feel. What Holy Spirit speaks is real. Holy Spirit shows you things to come and you must allow God's will to be done. You can't do anything without Him. He never forces Himself on you, always invite Him in and you will always win. There's no loosing in what He chooses.

Behold, behold, as the blessings unfold. Be ye also ready to hear, listen, do, and receive what has come and shall continue to come to you. Never be discouraged, but always be encouraged.

Sometimes you feel like things aren't coming fast enough. It's all in God's time. You shall shine in His divine. He made it this way so that you will not stray and blessings shall continue to come your way.

The people now see what God has done and it's marvelous in our sights. Today is the day of **RIP IT — Released Increase and Prosperity, I Take.**

Three days after your birthday. Three days Jesus Christ was raised from the dead. Three in one operating in your life. Father, Son, Holy Spirit. Blessings coming in three's. Large blessings that are promised to me.

I've been set in this large place, because what I'm receiving is not enough room to receive. God has set me here, and I have no fear. I shall forever be grateful and remain faithful.

My faith is now, and I thank God for Holy Spirit showing me how. I shall bless who God says bless. I receive far more than the rest. I continue to receive, because of my obedience. God people are waiting on me.

I love you God with all my heart, mind, soul, might, and spirit. Thank you God for always blessing me. I receive. I receive. The spirit of the lord is upon me. I live in health, wholeness, and wealth. God has pleasure in prospering me. I'm rejoicing and exceeding glad.

MAY 26, 2016

G.A.M.E.	P.I.C.
Grace	Phones
Anointing	Ipads
Manifestation	Computers
Encouraged	

Just like we invite people to play the games on our **Phones, iPads, and computers,** we should be quick to invite people to the kingdom of God. We want people to match our scores or just have fun with other players. We as the body of Christ should be excited to win souls, and be happy about the lost being found.

God gives this example of **GAME** and **PIC** for people to understand the importance of winning souls to the kingdom. This is Jesus' ministry. We are charged to follow his example. As we see examples throughout God's Word, we have the **Grace, Anointing, Manifestation,** and are **Encouraged** to do so, as God has the pleasure to prosper His people. In using our **Phones, iPads, and Computers,** we should make use of the tools given by man to advance the kingdom. God gives us gifts and talents to use for His kingdom's work, as the world has given material gifts for our pleasure or to stay in contact and communication with each other.

Holy Spirit is a gift from God that we receive when we ask and receive Him. He's our Game changer. We must invite Him in at all times, be excited to obey Him and get the work done in the kingdom and for our pleasure. This is our reward for kingdom work. As we seek the kingdom first and His righteousness, God adds everything else unto us.

We have different types of games to be played, as we have different types of people and situations needing changing or fixing: but all seeking one purpose, which is to win. Games that the world wants to win, and souls needing to be won to the kingdom.

We use our abilities, and strategies with different keys or applications on phones, iPads, and computers; as believers we should use our help from Holy Spirit by knowing his voice, speaking what he says, and obeying.

The price has been paid for by people for the different games or Apps: as the price has been paid by Jesus Christ to win souls back to their rightful place in God's kingdom. This is God's plan for mankind. We are always on God's mind, as this scripture tells us:

> *The Lord hath been mindful of us: he will bless us; he will bless the house of Israel; he will bless the house of Aaron.*
>
> Psalms 115:12 KJV

You have the **GAME** and **PIC** to assist. Keep working and allowing Holy Spirit to work through you and do what God says to do, and you will continue to receive all promises that's been given you, by Grace, through faith as our God has made away. This is what almighty God speaks as example for His people to understand what's important to Him.

JUNE 2, 2016

Never get off the path I've set you on. You are on this path to win. Never allow the enemy to make you take a different direction. Don't be afraid, know that this is the path I've made. I'm always with you. Make sure you do as I say to do.

When you see *danger, distraction, and destruction; never change your direction because of what you see.* This is a temporary, light affliction that didn't come from Me.

The enemy will follow you, as well as the saints. Just remember never to think you can't. You have passed through many dangerous roads. Don't panic when you see the enemy working and coming after you, I've prepared and showed you what to do. Pay attention always to what Holy Spirit shows you. Never let anyone else lead you, where I've shown you and appointed you to go.

Be patient and know that even when you recognize and see the enemy working, don't be afraid. Stand still and know that I am God. I'm your protection, even when it seems like there's no one coming to your rescue. Know that the blood of Jesus shall always cover you. Don't stop confessing, "The blood of Jesus covers me."

I hear what you speak, I come when you cry or call. Never follow those who I caused you to lead. Suggestions are good, and made in good faith, but I set you in this race. Never let anyone get you out of place. If you get afraid and run away, know that the people following, trust you and know that I'm covering you, and you know what to do. Again, keep confessing, "The blood of Jesus covers me," and the enemy has to flee.

He tries to rob you of what he sees on you. The blood of Jesus is on, in, and covering you. My blood runs through your veins, in Jesus' name — the name that's above every name. The name that never changes. The Word that stays the same. The Word that was made flesh, and dwells among the rest. The Word that made you My best. The Word that allowed you to pass tests.

You are anointed, and appointed to finish the work I've called you to do. You are royal, and wearing the diamonds and dominion I've given to you. It's My pleasure to prosper you. I am that I am, the Almighty, all-powerful God. I never make a mistake.

This I do for you is first for the kingdom sake. Because you are concerned that the kingdom never goes without, I've blessed you and your house. Know that no one else brought this about. The people will see and it will be marvelous in their sights, they will know what, I The Lord, your God and their God has done.

JUNE 10, 2016

Never let life situations make you live any way but righteously. Never say you can't. Never hide behind anything or anyone. Always make your presence known. Speak what Holy Spirit has shown. You were made to shine, in God's divine. It's your time.

God uses those who are willing and obedient. You are a front and forward person, pressing and pushing toward the mark of the prize of the higher calling in Christ Jesus, who went to the cross, died, and rose again for remission of your sins that have been forgiven. The way has been made. The price was paid.

The Spirit reveals the deeper things of God. You know the Spirit of God by praying in the spirit, with the evidence of speaking in tongues. What I call comes. Mountains are removed and casted into the sea. Walls are down. When the devil says no, God says yes. God is an awesome God.

You are in control because God placed you here on earth to have dominion over all things. Continue praising God as He adds to His church daily, such as to be saved. Nations are saved because of your words spoken, obedience, love, and worshipping God in Spirit and in truth.

You allowed yourself to be sought out by God. New and next level of praise has caused these steps to be made. *Functioning, fruitful, faithful, and favor in finances. Healing, hope and harvest.* Never stop what God has set in motion for you, which are these *series of events, experiences, encouragement, efficiency, ever increasing, supernatural, unlimited supply of His blessings.*

JUNE 11, 2016

Let nothing stop you from doing what I told you to do. You have been placed in this position to pray, praise, and prophesy. Teach, preach, and reach the Unreachable. Love, unconditionally.

Hear Me at all times when I speak. Never have a mind that's clogged and not clear to hear. I have released people to hear Me, to bring you favor without labor. Your job is to be in place, so they can see your face. They have heard your name, and I have caused them to see your face. Now they can say you are the one I have called to Pastor the church and help take them to new levels in Christ Jesus.

Always have ears to hear what My Spirit has to say to you. This is why you can't just do what you want to do. Keep your mind on Me, as I keep you in perfect peace. This peace surpasses all your understanding. If you could have thought it, it would have been done already. Never do things on your own. I'm God, and God alone. This is My throne.

I have given you everything by grace, through faith. I've made the way, even when you couldn't see your way. These blessings I've released are first for My kingdom, and then your house. You will never go empty. You will never have lack. I've brought you back. You are on track. Don't concentrate on the attack. You have won, because of My Son.

Don't look at what you can't see right now, Holy Spirit will continue to show you how. Stay in place. Go where I say to go, even where you don't know. When I say go, just go, don't ask questions or try and figure it out. Know that I caused this to come about. Continue to hear, listen, and do as Holy Spirit speaks to you.

In the next few days the plans will be made. You must obey what I say. Get in position. Open your eyes, ears, heart, and mind, and you will shine in My Divine — it's your time. I know you've been discouraged, now be encouraged. Never let the enemy take you there. Always bring your thoughts into subjection to Me.

Never touch or think anything because of your fleshly desires. Your desires must be line with Mine. Train and tell your mind what to do according to My will for you. I have set in motion for you to receive your portion. Share with others what I have set in your path and presence.

The gospel has to be carried out, that's why I've chosen you. You are willing and obedient; therefore you are eating the good of the land. This is all in My plans. You have the anointing on you and the oil in your hands. I'm the God that has chosen to use man and woman. I never make a mistake. This is done for Christ's sake. Live right at all times.

In the end you shall see Me. I've made you in My image. Live from the inside out. Know what's in the spirit realm. What's in the inside will show up on the outside. In the natural realm people will see the outside first, then receive what you will give them that comes from the inside.

Be careful how you look. Don't be dressed up on the outside and messed up on the inside.

Ask Yourself These Seven "Are You" Questions

1) Are you looking good on the outside, but sickness and disease is killing your inside?
2) Are you smiling on the outside, but crying on the inside?
3) Are you looking wealthy on the outside, but broke inside your purse and wallet?
4) Are you looking like you are innocent and can be trusted on the outside, but you are a liar and deceiver on the inside?
5) Are you saying you love people from the outside, but inside you have no love?
6) Are you quoting scriptures to people outside, but not living them inside?
7) Are you saying you love God, but inside your heart you don't even know Him?

Know these 7 things that you are from God!

1) You are a spiritual and natural being, fearfully and wonderfully made.
2) You are made in His image.
3) You are living life the way that He's has made you to be, from the inside out.
4) You are loving like He loves.
5) You are living righteously.
6) You are willing and obedient and eating the good of the land.
7) You have wealth and riches in your house.

You are built to last. Know that lasting is from what you have built. I've created you to have dominion, be fruitful, subdued, and replenished. Everything I've told you to do, you must walk in it. Believe, trust, rely on Me, and receive all that I've promised, positioned, and placed you here for. Prosperity is from Me, because it gives Me pleasure. I am your almighty, all-powerful God. Hear Me as I speak. Enjoy!

JUNE 11, 2016

Get GCW back going. Keep flowing, even in the not knowing. You are still growing. Stay in place. Don't get out of the race. You are not off beat. I put the running in your feet. Continue running.

I have given you plenty of money. You are living in this land that flows with milk and honey. This is the land of no scarceness. No lack. You are on track. You breeze through every attack. Everything the enemy has stolen I have given it back.

Victories, victories, victories, and vindication, I have set you before nations. People will hear and see, all that only comes from Me. The rhythm is in the running of the race; make sure you keep up the pace. You will never fall on your face. All is done for Christ's sake. I make no mistake.

I have sealed up the holes, with blessings untold. Every stone that was thrown I have used to build your home — this home that's built on a solid foundation.

Again, I have set you before nations. Speak my word. With Men, women, boys, and girls, you shall be heard. Pray the prayer of prophecy. Speak My word.

TLC

Throw the Line and Catch

Reel in the ones that grab hold, the ones that don't, let them go. No stress, struggle, or strain, you are in My vein. Never complain. Just do it all in My name. Your life will never be the same.

Your family, and friends who are faithfully connected to Me are connected to you. The doors are opened and doors are closed. The doors that were closed, I open them now. The doors that were not opened by Me, I close now. Enter into My *place of peace, promises, provisions, promotions, and prosperity.*

Know that I have done this for you. Why? My kingdom is at hand, and I need someone willing to stand. Follow My plans. Continue to stand. Keep worshipping me in spirit and in truth, and watch Me continue to make it happen for you.

Praise Me without hesitation, always from the heart. Loving Me is key, to all that keeps coming from Me. People will see how you love Me, and how I cause you to love them. Continue to pray, stay, and do it My way.

Pray for those who have gone astray and those whom I have told to stay. Pray for those who are doing things my way. I have prepared the people to assist with the tasks. They are waiting for the word I have sent through you by way of Holy Spirit. Step out. You have people waiting to help bring it about. Have no doubt. It's all been worked out.

Money is never a problem. Money shall keep coming, as people will keep growing and sowing. People will obey and release the money I have allowed to come their way. Money is here to stay. In your going out and your coming in, I'm blowing them in like a mighty rushing wind — quickly, suddenly.

The white fields are already harvested. The harvest is plenteous, but the laborers are few, just remember to keep doing what I say to do. There's no time for running in place, pick up the pace. It's all done for Christ's sake. He paid the price, the ultimate sacrifice. Now it's pay back time. Walk, in his divine as if your life is on the line. This is the word from your almighty, all-powerful, loving, unchanging God!

JUNE 13, 2016

God is preparing the sanctuary for us to walk in. He is awesome. People are welcoming with open arms. They have been waiting for this moment. Beautiful stained glass with chandelier is beyond the doors. Stairs lead up to the altar. There's a large beautiful stage and sanctuary.

We waited patiently. What we thought was, wasn't. Our desire was to help; however we never missed a step. We are back in line. We shine in God's divine. No more sideline. We have come from the back to the front. NOW! Never to fall behind again.

We win, because we overcame sin. We never go back, we stay on track. We never get out of line. We made it to the finish line. Our finish is a start to another destination. The souls just keep on coming. The power of God is resting on me. God has allowed me to see where He wants us to be.

Never get weary in well-doing. We have reaped because we fainted not. There's no failing in God, as we are made in His image. There's no failing in us. We are the chosen to take His church to new levels in Christ Jesus. Here we are, we didn't have to go far. The blessing was right in range and reach. We receive Now!

Holy Spirit will lead you and show you what, when, and where to go. Continue to flow, and follow. This fountain shall never run dry. God has given us supernatural abundant unlimited supply.

Obedience shall always be key. Teach the sheep. Love the sheep. Never manipulate the sheep. God has laid it all at our feet. It's ours for the asking. It's in God's will.

All our dreams have been fulfilled. Because we are concerned about the kingdom, and God has given us the kingdom. Kingdom bountiful blessings, resting, reigning, and ruling in you, because you have done and shall continue to do what God says to do.

God is pleased to prosper you. This is the Word from the almighty God!

JUNE 21, 2016

Revolving Doors

Doors are opening. As one swing open, another one opens. Continual doors opening, one after another. Never missing an entrance. I've been here before, through this door.

Go back and revisit where you thought you couldn't go at the time. It's time. Who told you that you couldn't walk in? In Him you have everything. You can do all things through Christ, which strengthens you.

Receive what looks like it's too much for you to afford. It's yours for the asking now. People have given you favor. It's all prepared for you, waiting for you to receive. They've been waiting on you. Go back fill out the application. You are approved.

Even though you don't have the money in your hands at the time. Money is released to you. Resources are released to you. Listen to what I say to do. Stay tuned into Holy Spirit channel. Channels of wealth. It's opened now. You don't know how, it's not for you to know, because you didn't allow the flow.

Stay in your lane. It's released in Jesus' name. Your heirship, you have. Money flows through the valves, loosened. Traveling to your house, from the bottom to the top. Money from the fish's mouth, open it and take it out.

Heathens have been holding onto what I've released to you. Receive now. Money that's been waiting for its rightful owner. You are the chosen one. The money has begun. Open up; let it in.

Remember I am the way, truth and the light, and I've brought this all about. Rejoice and be exceedingly glad. Receive more money than you ever had. You are supernaturally, abundantly supplied, unlimited money continuing to multiply. Enjoy it's my pleasure.

JUNE 27, 2016

#WhenWePray!

1) Superior God

2) Spiritual Gifts

3) Sufficient Grace

4) Sowing Giving

5) Spreading Gospel

6) Supernatural Growth

When we pray, we pray to a *Superior God*. We receive *Spiritual Gifts*, and *Sufficient Grace*. Our *Sowing and Giving* goes to another level. We are *Spreading the Gospel, and Supernatural Growth* takes place. When we pray, the heavens are open. We live the life that has been prepared, preserved, and promised us, to prosper by grace through faith. God always makes a way out of no way. God's wealth, wisdom, and Word is here to stay, when we pray.

Outsiders become insiders. We live from the inside out. We shout. Walls come down. Demons drown. God is always around.

You are never left alone. When we pray, storms pass — they can't stay. Valleys are open to pass through. We know what to do. Holy Ghost power is with you. We hear, listen, and do what God wants us to do.

When we pray, we are willing and obedient. We eat the good of the land, and we spend our days in prosperity and our years in pleasure. When we pray, we have healing, hope, harvest, and wholeness. Blessings flow and flood continually. We pray without ceasing.

When we pray, praise and worship are working together. The inside is working on the outside. Inside worship, bringing outside praise. Hands are lifted up. Shouting Hallelujah!!! Hallelujah!!! Hallelujah!!! Heart seated, saturated, spiritual and supernatural worship.

When we pray, we know God inhabits the praise of His people; and because of our praise, He adds to His church daily, such as to be saved.

When we pray, we worship God in spirit and in truth, for He seeks us out to worship Him.

When we pray, we know this is the time that the true worshippers come forth.

When we pray, we live righteous; knowing the effectual, fervent prayers of the righteous availeth much.

When we pray, we have a blood-bought right to answered prayers.

When we pray, we believe and trust, knowing God heard us the first time, as the prayers were spoken out of our mouths. According to His will, He has already granted the requests, by grace, through faith, it's done.

Victory, victory, after victory, we have won, because of His only Son, Jesus Christ, our Lord and saviour. Favor, favor, favor and no labor.

When we pray, we are spiritually minded, and we have life and peace. The spirit of the Lord is upon me. The blood covers me. Every day brand new mercies we receive.

When we pray, we speak, and sing, mightily this scripture:

Worthy is the Lamb who was slaughtered— to receive power and riches and wisdom and strength and honor and glory and blessing.

(Revelation 5:12 NLT)

**Don't just take notes but take notice!
You can't be blessed without giving!**

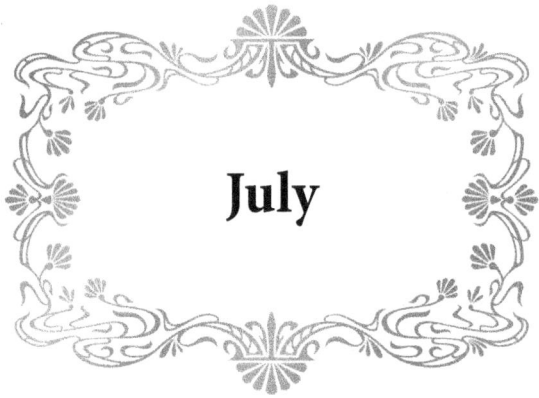

JULY 3, 2016

Greater works I've given thee, because you're following after Me. You reach beyond your reach even when you don't see. I bring back to your remembrance things that I've said, from the scriptures you've read. Always think thoughts of Me even when you go to bed. Remember I placed them in your head.

Receive and say yes. These things I speak are no longer a mystery, because I've revealed them to you. Holy Spirit shows you what to do. Obey what he has to say, because this is the only way.

Love never fails, as you continue to sail and supersede in supernatural blessings from Me. You've asked according to My will, and it's done unto you. Never cease to follow after Me. Stay in My presence, regardless of what you see. What you see is not necessarily what you will get. If you see lack, don't accept it as truth, I shall always provided for you. Never get out of place, I've set you here for people to see your face. It might seem strange to you, it's what I have told you to do. You might seem like you out of place, you are not. Where you are going I've not forgot.

You are here to be recognized for these seven kingdom reasons.
1) Kingdom Mantel for Display
2) Kingdom Man for Dominion
3) Kingdom Mind for Domain
4) Kingdom Ministry for Deliverance
5) Kingdom Marriage for Demonstration
6) Kingdom Money for Demand
7) Kingdom Manifestation for Doing

You are here on the *Kingdom Mantle for Display* because I've called *Kingdom Man and Woman for Dominion,* and with your *Kingdom Mind for Domain* as everything is brought to your remembrance, which I've placed in your brain. Retain and receive the *Kingdom Ministry for Deliverance* of all those who will and want to be saved.

Your *Kingdom Marriage is for Demonstration,* for all others to know that even though things happened that wasn't of Me. I have allowed you to fix what you've broken. Always do what I've already spoken.

Kingdom Money is for Demand and in My plans. You shall receive *Kingdom Manifestation for doing* everything as unto Me. Receive revelations as you follow after Me, this is the way it shall be.

Again, know that you are here for the people to see. This is marvelous for all the world to see, that I've made this happen, for the kingdom is in need. Stay focused on the Kingdom *increase, impartation, information, instructions, and inspiration.* I've set you here before the nations. Rejoice and be exceedingly glad. More souls keep on coming to the kingdom, and only the devil is mad.

Money keeps on coming for the kingdom and your house, never doubt. I've brought you out, from the back to the front. Continue to do for the kingdom, and I continue to do for you. I'm your almighty, all-powerful God.

JULY 20, 2016

Let everything that Apostle Dr. Leroy Thompson spoke at Camp Meeting 2016 sink in. Go into the fields knowing that the fields are already harvested. Don't delay; your help is here today. Do and receive what you heard Apostle say. Get the apostolic seals down in your spirit.

Pray in the spirit like you've never done before. Walk in every opened door. It's already been done. Every door I shut, don't try to go back in.

Remember to let everything sink in because you always win. Your time has come. Ministries are birthing through you. People are attracted to you. It's the anointing they're drawn to. Stay focused and in faith. Know that I made it this way.

Piles and piles of money have been released to you. Receive the six blessings that were awaiting your arrival when you returned home. Hidden blessings are revealed and shown, because of the unknown.

Miracle working power is here; it's my atmosphere. Walk in. Never look back because you are on track. There can never be any more lack. Just when you think your money is short, money just keeps on coming to you. You don't know how or when, just keep expecting money to come in. Why? Because you seek My kingdom first, and My righteousness, and all things shall continue to be added unto you.

Never give up and never give in. Again, just allow what was spoken to constantly and continually sink in. This is My love show. I show off in you, when you obey and serve Me.

Continue to walk into the fields of harvest. Every crop you see come up, know it's from Me. Every dead grass, you must keep walking past. If it looks like a weed, know that it's not from My seed.

I minister seed to the sower. What I give grows. The wheat and tares grow together, but I do the separating. Plant My seeds, and nurture and water them with the words of Holy Ghost coming from your mouth. Then, look for the harvest. You can't receive what you're not looking for.

Continue doing what I say and all these blessings shall continue to come your way. I'm blowing them in like a mighty rushing wind. This wind you can't see, but you will know the effects come only from Me.

See your *ministry, it's mightier* than ever before. See you *marriage*, it's *mounted* and *made* stronger than ever before. See your *money*, it's *manifesting* and just keeps on *moving* to you like never before.

Yes, keep letting it sink in, I know it's a lot, and plenty more is coming in. Pay attention, be attentive, follow *instructions,* because I have *imparted increase* like never before.

Again, walk in the doors. You have heard what I said through Apostle Dr. Leroy Thompson. I never go back on My Word. The blessings just keep on coming to you. Money just keeps on coming to you. Continue to hear, listen and do. I've made it all happen for you. Believe My prophets, so shall you continue to prosper. It's My pleasure. I am, that I am, your almighty, all-powerful God!

JULY 26, 2016

Using the sky as an example of what God says.

When the sky is dark and cloudy, know that I am God almighty. Know that I have the power to turn your dark and dead situations into light and living in Christ Jesus. When the sky is gray and you can't see your way, know that I am the God that can change your situations any day.

When the sky is clear and blue, know that I am the God that has made all these blessings come to you. Receive what you see, when you receive what I say. When I say no, don't make it a yes. You have been set apart from the rest, because you are My very elect, and have passed the tests.

The effects of the sky and the clouds brings the outcome here on the ground. The dark and gloomy clouds bring rain, which removes the dryness of the dirt. When the dirt is nurtured, fertilized, and watered with the rain it brings forth green grass. When I am speaking from heaven, and you are hearing and listening, by way of Holy Spirit and doing what it takes in the natural, you shall receive the supernatural.

I've created all things and given them to you. Male and female. Man from the dirt of the earth and woman from man's rib, and not man from man's rib. I created he and she, and made them be, but the enemy made them listen and like what didn't come from Me.

The sky is your example and explanation of what you have seen, are seeing, and shall continue to see. Pay attention. Follow the instructions that I have already given you. Obey Holy Spirit because he will speak to you, through you, and for you.

Hear, listen and do everything I've spoken to you. You will continue to receive everything that's been promised to you.

JULY 29, 2016

When we Seek God **EARLY**,
- **E**nemies are
- **A**nnihilated we
- **R**eceive
- **L**ove and
- **Y**ears of Prosperity

He opens up heaven, and we receive here on **EARTH**,
- **E**verything
- **A**nointing
- **R**evelations
- **T**ruths
- **H**oly Ghost Power

We are not trapped and stuck solely with what God has said, but what He's saying. We are not totally focusing on what He's done, but what He's doing. We're not stopping at what He has given us, but what He's continually giving us. Never cease or stop praying, praising, and worshipping God in spirit and in truth, along with asking for His help.

We must rise **early**. Things happen and we are *released, rewarded, and we reign* in seeking God in our **early** rising. Seeking Him **early** causes us to fast, while asking for His help.

Our enemies are defeated and we receive their possessions. We have no need to fear or fight. We set ourselves, stand still, and see the salvation of the Lord. We know that our God is with us, and the battle is not ours, but His. We are chosen leaders and believers of God.

In our praise and worship of Him, we must bow low with our face to the ground before Him, as we are the examples, which cause others to follow and do the same. Together our **early** rising, going forth, and worshipping God with a loud voice has brought about the total destruction of our enemies.

As God's prophets, we have been given the power and authority to speak and appoint singers who praise the beauty and holiness of our awesome God. His mercy and truth endures forever. We must believe the Lord our God, then are we established. As we believe His prophets, we shall prosper.

Finally we must receive all that God has given us because of our **early** rising and seeking Him and asking for His help. Out of our obedience to Him and believing His prophets, we not only receive prosperity, but we also receive overflowing, outpouring and overtaking of His blessings.

There are times we can pray, praise, and worship God in the noonday and throughout the day: however, by rising **early,** seeking, praising and worshiping our God, we do the *unusual, uncomfortable, uncommon,* and we receive the *unusual, unlimited, unconditional,* blessings which only come from heaven's open doors.

We must start receiving here on earth what has been released in these set times of favor, because of our obedience, love, and faithfulness to God at all times. He's the one who causes us to shine in His divine. The light of His favor, fruits, and finances continues to shine bright and never goes dim, as we continue to believe and trust Him. See confirmation of His Word in the scriptures below.

> *And Jehoshaphat feared, and set himself to seek the Lord, and proclaimed a fast throughout all Judah. And Judah gathered themselves together, to ask help of the Lord: even out of all the cities of Judah they came to seek the Lord.*
>
> *Behold, I say, how they reward us, to come to cast us out of thy possession, which thou hast given us to inherit.*

And he said, Hearken ye, all Judah, and ye inhabitants of Jerusalem, and thou king Jehoshaphat, Thus saith the Lord unto you, Be not afraid nor dismayed by reason of this great multitude; for the battle is not yours, but God's.

Ye shall not need to fight in this battle: set yourselves, stand ye still, and see the salvation of the Lord with you, O Judah and Jerusalem: fear not, nor be dismayed; to morrow go out against them: for the Lord will be with you. And Jehoshaphat bowed his head with his face to the ground: and all Judah and the inhabitants of Jerusalem fell before the Lord, worshipping the Lord. And the Levites, of the children of the Kohathites, and of the children of the Korhites, stood up to praise the Lord God of Israel with a loud voice on high. And they rose early in the morning, and went forth into the wilderness of Tekoa: and as they went forth, Jehoshaphat stood and said, Hear me, O Judah, and ye inhabitants of Jerusalem; Believe in the Lord your God, so shall ye be established; believe his prophets, so shall ye prosper. And when he had consulted with the people, he appointed singers unto the Lord, and that should praise the beauty of holiness, as they went out before the army, and to say, Praise the Lord; for his mercy endureth for ever. And when they began to sing and to praise, the Lord set ambushments against the children of Ammon, Moab, and mount Seir, which were come against Judah; and they were smitten.

And when Jehoshaphat and his people came to take away the spoil of them, they found among them in abundance both riches with the dead bodies, and precious jewels, which they stripped off for themselves, more than they could carry away: and they were three days in gathering of the spoil, it was so much.

2 Chronicles 20:3-4, 11, 15, 17-22, KJV

AUGUST 8, 2016

1) Peace is a Plus
2) Prosperity is a Promise
3) Position is a Place

This things are from heaven and in you on earth.

1) **My Peace is a Plus.**

    Know that My perfect peace is in you as along as you keep your mind on Me. I give you peace that surpasses all understanding.

2) **Prosperity is a Promise.**

    When you believe My prophets, so shall you receive prosperity. All My promises are yes and Amen. Say yes and agree with Me for all you see and shall continue to see that I've already brought to pass in your life. Receive your Ephesians 3:20 blessings now.

Now unto him that is able to do exceeding abundantly above all that we ask or think, according to the power that worketh in us.

(Ephesians 3:20 KJV)

3) **Position is a Place.**

This Position is a Place in Christ Jesus that I've given you to hear, listen, and do everything I've said to do, and shall continue to speak to you, by way of Holy Spirit. All these three can only come from Me, your almighty, all-powerful God. I've been with you from the start, because you have My heart. You are My beloved ones. You are here for a reason; this is your season. Your time has come, because of My Son.

My kingdom is in need, and I've blessed you indeed. Everything around you, everywhere you go and everywhere you haven't traveled has been enlarged. I've set you in this large place, and you receive when you obey what I say. Houses and lands are in My plans, and I've placed them all in your hands. Continue to stand. Living right is the key, if you don't, you won't receive what's been released from Me.

I've

1) **Rescued** you from the hands of the enemy. You must always
2) **Recognize,** who I am and who's child you are. If you get off track, remember
3) **Repentance,** is a must, if you want to receive My stuff.

When you continue to obey and serve Me, live in righteousness, love Me with all your might and soul; then you can never be in,

1) **Poverty and Living Homeless,**

2) **Poor and Losing Health, or**

3) **In Prison and Left Hanging.**

In all that you do, always live out this scripture, I've given you.

> *But seek ye first the kingdom of God, and his righteousness; and all these things shall be added unto you.*
>
> (Matthew 6:33 KJV)

You have your keys, now unlock all these blessings I've given thee. There are things that you won't have to pray for because of your *seeking, serving, surroundings, set apart, spiritual, and supernatural supply, that have come from heaven to you, My holy and righteous servants*. Receive and live now in this scripture I've given you:

> *Blessed be the God and Father of our Lord Jesus Christ, who hath blessed us with all spiritual blessings in heavenly places in Christ:*
>
> (Ephesians 1:3 KJV)

> *Now, because of these two scriptures I've given you have the right to receive.*
>
> *The earth is the LORD's, and everything in it. The world and all its people belong to him.*
>
> *They will receive the LORD's blessing and have a right relationship with God their savior.*
>
> (Psalms 24:1, 5 NLT)

You have My dominion and you are living in My kingdom's blessings, doing My kingdom's work, and living out My Word in this scripture.

> *For we are his workmanship, created in Christ Jesus unto good works, which God hath before ordained that we should walk in them.*
>
> (Ephesians 2:10 KJV)

Rejoice and be exceedingly glad. Again, receive all these blessings you never had. It's My pleasure to give you My treasures. Enjoy!!!

AUGUST 6, 2016

Connected with the word from 7/29/2016

Power House
Promises from Heaven
Pleasing Him
Personal Helper

I got the Power in my House. I Receive my Promises from Heaven. I'm Pleasing to Him. Holy Spirit is my Personal Helper. He shows me how, what, when, and who to listen to. I do as he says to do, everything as unto the Lord.

Blessings, blessings, and blessings have been released because of the kingdom's sake. I seek the kingdom daily and His righteousness and all these things have been added unto me. I've received by grace through faith all these blessings that keep rolling my way, day after day, because I obey, what God has to say.

My willingness and obedience has caused me to dwell in the land, and verily I'm fed. I continue to live out what God has said. I always know and do what He's saying. I'm living in the overflow. I continue to go and grow.

People continue to sow. They give unto me and I give unto Thee. All that I have and all that I am is because God has made it this way. Open up, open up, I walk in, and through the Red Sea that's been opened up for me. It's all provided for me.

Before time became time, it's all mine. I shine in His divine. The dim isn't dark, instead it's become bright and shines like the light. It's on. People see what God has done through His Son. Jesus is my lover. My unconditional love. I hear, listen, and do what's been spoken. As the earth was created and made, it's all about me, given to me to have dominion, and dominate over.

I multiply, I subdue, and I replenish. I'm spiritual minded. I have life and peace. Nothing shall harm me. I'm protected by the blood of Jesus, because I'm doing it all in Christ Jesus' name — my reason for these seasons of harvest.

The crops have come up. I'm the stuff. Even when things get rough, I'm tough. I always have more than enough. I never back down. Everything my hand touches prospers. My businesses prosper.

Tomorrow is a day of increase, because of the release. Because of the kingdom's blessings, *impartation, inspiration, and influence* has begun. People shall see and say, **"Look what God has done."** God is all-knowing, all-powerful, almighty, and loving.

I'm tuned in. Channels of wealth and health are here. This is the atmosphere. I Receive God's best. He's set me apart from the rest. I've passed the tests.

Nothing is impossible. All things are possible, because of your belief in Me. **I am, that I am has spoken.** I am His, and I know this, and I receive it all. I'm rejoicing and exceedingly glad. I'm enjoying. Thank you Lord, my God.

AUGUST 23, 2016

Things we can't do, and must do to receive from God

1) Blend With the Sinners

2) Blind Weak and Serving

3) Bold Workers and Stand out

4) Bind Work of Satan

5) Believe Word of the Saviour

6) Blessings Wealth and Supernatural

We must trust and believe this scripture:

> *But ye are a chosen generation, a royal priesthood, an holy nation, a peculiar people; that ye should shew forth the praises of him who hath called you out of darkness into his marvelous light:*
>
> 1 Peter 2:9 KJV

Therefore we can't *Blend With the Sinners*, however we should be *Bold Workers and Standout*. We absolutely must not be *Blind Weak and Serving* our almighty, most high God. The one who allows us to be all that He has *chosen, called, commissioned, charged, and commanded* us to be. The one who is, and shall always be, with us and for us; and we never have to worry about who's against us.

We must continue to *Bind Work of Satan.* **He has to be cast out, and not just called out in prayer. We can't pray him away,** because at the end of the day, we gotta know he's trying to stay.

When we *Believe the Word of the Saviour,* we live a life of favor and no labor. *Blessings Wealth and Supernatural Surplus,* and all sufficiency come from God Himself. When we know all these things; and that we are picked out with a plan and purpose from God, we will want to do what's pleasing in His sight.

We have been brought into the light. We must shine in His divine at all times. Make up our minds. Never allow the temporary darkness to allow our light to go dim or dark. Just like if your lights get shut off in your home, you know it's temporary light affliction, only for a moment, and they will be turned back on.

Know that nothing must keep your light from shining bright, because God has made things better and beyond all right. We must see beyond what's been broken from you, because of His Son. The blessings of royalty, and holiness are upon you. Continue to hear, listen and do everything God says to do, and His blessings shall keep on flowing and keep on coming to you. Keep Him in your heart; never let Him depart. Love is the most important part. I decree my love for God is never-ending. I'm rejoicing and exceedingly glad.

AUGUST 26, 2016

We can't resist the favorable deal that God has prepared for us. Never settle for less, because He has given us His best.

Lord, I thank you for this land that flows with milk and honey and plenty of money.

Lord, I thank you that I never let the enemy distract me.

Lord, I thank you for money that just keeps on coming to me.

Lord, I thank you for all this money that you allowed to prosper me.

Lord, I thank you for great health and wealth: and even my soul prospers.

Lord, I thank you for your prophets that have spoken your Word. I believe your prophets and so am I prospering.

I never think small because God has given me all. All of His promises is a yes and Amen. I agree with Him for all He has for me, and I receive. I am in place and I hear what God has to say. I am there. I am a God-made miracle millionaire. I see all these blessings on me.

I come before God in total nakedness and I allow Him to dress me. I'm dressed in the garments of praise as I bless His holy name. I know His name is always the same and He never changes.

I have on my shoes of peace and I go where He says to go. I have on my robe of righteousness, but I never cease to seek His kingdom first, while all these things have been added unto me. I worship God from the inside, until the praise comes out!

I continue walking in my shoes of peace, because the Spirit of the Lord is upon me. I stay covered with my robe of righteousness, and allow Him to keep giving to me, as I'm receiving His best. People will see and say that only God could have done this for me.

I'm the example here on earth; this fullness that is His and He's given to us. I love living this life of plenty. Needs, I don't have any, because God has already supplied. Wants and desires of my heart have been given in dominion.

I'm fruitful, multiplying, replenishing, and subduing. *Unlimited resources, revenue, riches and wealth is in my house.* All because we are God's beloved ones. All because of His Son. I'm living in Christ Jesus. Yes, this is the reason. This is my season. I'm receiving all the time.

Just like seasons continue year 'round, so do my blessings. Unlimited, never stopping, can't count them. I'm rejoicing, exceedingly glad. I'm living better than I ever have. Thank you almighty, all-powerful God.

AUGUST 31, 2016

1/29/2016 First Spoken
A mighty move of God! The move is on!

God has spoken. It's moving time. We are walking in God's divine. Holy Spirit has prompted me to call on the Angels. They are on assignment for us.

They are ministering and continue to minister to the board and members of our new church home. I have called, commissioned, and commanded the innumerable Angels to go, and they are on assignment for us now. They have heard the word from God spoken from my mouth, to move on our behalf now.

Release has taken place. The board and members have heard, by way of Holy Spirit, and the Angels have brought it to pass. Pastor AD and I are the chosen of God to lead this church of thousands of members to the next level in the kingdom of God. They have turned from their way of thinking and heard from God by way of the ministering angels. We have heard from the prophets and now we are prospering and the kingdom is prospering because of our obedience and the people of God obedience.

The move is on. We are moving into our new church and new property. We receive. The spirit of the Lord is upon me. We went through this for a reason. We learned and have earned. We now have testimonies of times, places, and manifestation. Thank you God for this mighty move.

The wind has blown the doors open. Angels have come in. I receive my visitation and manifestation. This is a quick move. Demonstration has taken place, because we are a kingdom generation. Generations and generations to come. The move is on.

Victory, victory, victory, has been won. Thank God for His Son. I'm never afraid, because this move God has allowed to be made. He's not a man. It's all in His plans. He's placed it all in our hands. We follow the process and receive our positions.

God is pleased to prosper His people. Thank you, God, for this large place of promotion and promises. We never stress, struggle, or strain, because God has brought the reign. We are *resting, ruling, rendering, refreshed, restored, and receiving* it all for the kingdom's sake and for our sakes.

I see, I see, what God wants me to see. I hear, listen and do everything unto God. We never forget from where God has brought us. We follow instructions. We have the impartation, like the same grace as our mentors. Never missing a move or moment of our time travels and destinations that have been set up for us by God. We are going far. This move has topped the bar. No barrier blockers, however bountiful blessings.

Continue, continue, continue, all this have become new. "The blessings of the Lord are upon you." This says our almighty, all-powerful God.

These words I speak are not my own, but from the One who owns this heaven we are experiencing right here on earth. I receive, I receive, I receive. Thank you, God, for the spirit of the Lord shall continue to be upon me.

Thank God for the four winds of His Holy Spirit. I receive all these that were spoken in the scriptures.

> *Saying with a loud voice, Worthy is the Lamb that was slain to receive power, and riches, and wisdom, and strength, and honour, and glory, and blessing.*
>
> Revelation 5:12 KJV

September

SEPTEMBER 3, 2016

I am the God of peace. I have sanctified you and made you holy. You are set apart from the rest. You are My very best. I have *cut every cord, connection, and communication that's not conducive to Me*. No longer will you choose who you connect or communicate with; I choose. **I am that I am.**

I have worked a work in you. I have completed this work. In Christ Jesus is where you are and what you do. My grace is sufficient for thee. It's already done by My grace through faith. Never stop the mixing of the two. I have provided for you. No one can change what I allow to remain.

The reign won't come without the preparation and expectation. Prepare to receive. Expect, believe and receive all the blessings that have come and shall continue to come from Me. Mighty moves in the spirit have been released and shall continue to be released here on earth. Speak the blessings and not the curses. Know that your *connections, conversations, and communication* are very important.

Never speak what I haven't spoken or what I'm not speaking. Never speak just what you want, but what I have said and continue to say. Never speak what you don't want, but what you do want, and what I want for you. Hear, listen, and do all that I say to do. Live in obedience, love, power, and righteousness. Keep seeking My kingdom and righteousness you will receive all these things I have added and continue to multiply and give to you.

There's no lack in My kingdom and no lack in your house. Only wealth and riches reside in your house. Only you can evict it all out. Watch what you speak out of your mouth. I have washed all filthy, corrupt communication out.

Know your enemy. Never allow them in. Never go back to who and what you have been delivered from. Just because they appear to be godly, you are only seeing the form. Again, never go back to what you have been delivered from. I repeat, because this is a very important key. This and they will cause you to be pulled away from Me.

My spirit I allowed you to discern. This you didn't earn. I have given you My grace. Now, receive through faith. I shall continue to lead the way. I have taken you to another place. This place is large. It's bigger than the people you try to connect and communicate with. They can't see or receive. Stay in place.

Know that I have allowed you to be in the race. Keep up the pace. Never fall on your face. You are on track. Never turn or look back. *Remember the cord had to be cut at birth. I have cut the cord, connection, and communication of those who aren't conducive and conformed to receive in the new birth I have given you.* Remember what I said. **I'm doing a new thing in 2016.**

I never change, because I'm not a man. I never lie. I created this earth with My Words; even though the darkness existed, I spoke light, and it came. You are made in My image, you can do the same. You can create with the words I have given you. When darkness exist or comes, speak light. When dead situations try to exist or come, speak life. I have given you dominion, fruitfulness, subduing, replenishing, and I allow things to multiply.

Remember the revelation spoken. You are making it with the words of your mouth. Be a doer, not just a hearer. Use the tools I have equipped you with, and you can't loose. Once words come out, you can't take them back in.

Repentance is turning and learning. Never repeating the lesson you've already passed. **Again, I am that I am; I have spoken.** I am The Almighty, all-powerful God. My Word is *the final Word* of all. Receive. "I receive." This is the Word of The Lord!

SEPTEMBER 3, 2016

It's Time to Receive!

All these blessings that have been given me! Blessings after blessings, blessings after blessings, blessings after blessings, I receive. God is showing off in me. Tell the people to receive what they see. Don't talk about me, or be jealous of what they see. Their time is coming, when they celebrate with me. Quickly, suddenly, this is how it shall be. "Receive this prophecy from Me," your almighty, all-powerful God.

Time never waits on anyone or anything. See the blessings I continue to bring, as I have given you everything. Receive. It's My pleasure, don't try and measure. *Unlimited, unloading, and unfolding blessings coming to me.* Again, receive all these blessings from Me.

I'm the truth, the way, and the light. You must love Me with all your might. Continue to give Me your heart and I will never depart. To receive, you must believe and trust Me. Believe My prophets that have spoken, are speaking, and shall continue to speak. I have revealed, I am revealing, and shall continue to reveal My secrets to My servants, the prophets.

Knowing that I shall do nothing except I reveal the secrets to them. Never listen to those prophets without revelation and information that never comes to pass. When what they speak comes to pass, then you know that I have sent them. Those that go their way, never listen to what they have to say. When they say "I think this", quickly turn your back, because they are off track. Know the ones that I have sent, there's no turning back, they are on track.

You shall never be in lack. When you believe My prophets, so shall you prosper. All that I do is because I love you. You are My beloved ones. Receive what I have done. Victories you have won, because of My Son. The price has been paid. Never put Christ Jesus back in the grave. Always live in Christ Jesus because of this very reason. The death, burial, and resurrection of My Son, and saviour was for those who received salvation. The world knows and sees him not. Shout, shout, shout, now receive everything I have allowed to come about. This is the Word of the Lord.

SEPTEMBER 14, 2016

Wisdom comes from God. If any man lacks wisdom, let him ask. Wisdom must never depart. Wisdom from God is never far. Never think on your own, because of God on His throne. Holy Spirit gives wisdom, allowing you to know where you belong. Never give up your power. This is God's finest hour.

Hear, listen, and do what has been spoken to you. Now you know what to do. *Receive resources, render services — that's what you are called to do.* Serve, pay attention to your surroundings. **Never go a day without being in the presence of the Lord.** When wisdom speaks, listen.

Holy Spirit is your avenue, God is your avenger. Walk down His avenue; you know what to do. Just do it. The power of God is resting on you.

Come in. Take your place. I've set you in this large place. Never be moved by what people do. I'm more than this world, which could be against you. Hear Me, your almighty, all-powerful God.

Work the work I've called you to. Never be afraid. Remember, when I spoke this world was made. In My image, you stay. Revelations come to you today. My blessings never go away. Nothing happens until the secrets are revealed.

What I've spoken, you have heard. What I'm speaking and shall continue to speak, you will continue to hear. Keep praying in the Spirit. Wisdom is what you shall hear. Righteousness is the way you live. Love is in your heart. Love is spread abroad.

Stay in My presence. Follow My plans. You have the blessings in your hands. Prosperity is in your land. Receive. I've given you the houses and land — this land that flows with milk and honey and plenty of money.

Always remember the mission. Know your motivation. Love Me. Receive. The manifestations are moving. Receive. You are in position. Receive. I've provided you with all My promises. Receive. I've sent people to give you favor without labor. They are excited to help you. Receive. Overflow is here. Again, you are there. You are My God-made miracle millionaire. Receive.

People will marvel at what I've done for you. I'm showing off in and through you. Always do exactly as I say to do. Speak what Holy Spirit speaks to and through you. You are set, because I put you in the race. The finish is done. You have won. When the rain comes, it pours, and it's a good thing for you. *You are flooding and flourishing in the fruitfulness and faithfulness of my finances.*

Just like Apostle Dr. Leroy Thompson has spoken, you believe. Now, receive. It's your time. It's your season. This has been done for kingdom reasons. You receive the overflow because you help the kingdom grow. You are living large, keep loving Me with all your heart. This is key.

You have the keys. Welcome. Doors are open. Come in. Sit with Me. The keys are from Me. They are to show your ownership. They are not needed to open these doors at this time.

Dine, shine in My divine. Again, it's your time. I've made it this way. Obey. Never get out of place by doing things your way, and your blessings shall be here to stay. It's My pleasure to prosper you. Receive. Rejoice and be exceedingly glad. This is the Word from the Lord!

SEPTEMBER 14, 2016

I hear the ticking of time deep down in my mind. Listen carefully, don't miss the sound. Don't miss what's being said. Don't be scared. Believe what you read. It's not just a sound in your head. Even though the sound might have faded away, believe what you heard today.

Receive. You will never be broke another day in your life. Money is always searching for you. You know what to do now! Continue to listen and hear the sound. Do what Holy Spirit says to do. Money miracles shall keep coming to you.

Your motivation is mission-minded. You have marriage mission, ministry mission, and money mission. Always pay attention to what you hear, have no fear. Stay in faith. The blessings will keep coming your way, and shall continue to stay. Holy Spirit will keep showing you how to function.

The sound is key. Know that it comes from Me. When you hear the sound, know that I'm around. Again, listen carefully as Holy Spirit speaks to you from Me. I am the almighty, all-sufficient, all-powerful God.

With Me revelations, resources, revenue, shall never depart. Always love Me with all your heart. You are strong and you live long. You are never just holding on. That is not your song. You have a song of praise as you bless the Lord's Holy name. Worship Me in Spirit and in truth. Why? Because I allow My Spirit to always be with you.

Receive. Receive. Receive. All that comes from Me. This is the Word of the Lord!

SEPTEMBER 16, 2016

Pop goes the weasel

Crops have come up because of the seeds sown, blessings that we haven't known and we didn't do on our own. Seeds continue to be ministered to you. Again, hear, listen, and do. Never sow where you don't know. I will tell you where to go and sow. Never go on your own. You are My seed pushers. You can never sow blind because I'm on your mind.

No one can steal what I've revealed. I give you brand-new revelations every day. I give you brand-new mercies every day, because you do things My way. Love never fails, and failing never stops the love.

I've given you dreams and visions. Go back to the dreams. Remember what you have seen. Mediate on them. Ask Holy Spirit to bring back the dreams that I've caused you to see. Even the daydreams. Write down the dreams you have seen and continue to see from Me. I have revealed hidden secrets in the dreams, and shall continue to reveal.

Dreams that are bad are warnings to you to fix the soul situations. They allow you to see where you are. I'm never far. I never leave or forsake you. Never be afraid of your dreams. I shall always allow you to know what they mean. You are a dream interpreter.

I've given you another gift to add to the many gifts. Dream big! Your dreams have already been released. You have the gift to know what they mean. Others have been asking you what their dreams mean. Think back to years ago. You wondered why people asked you about their dreams. Again, you know what they mean.

Never allow anyone to take what I have given you. Always keep your mind stayed on Me. People recognize your gifts. I have allowed them to see now, every gift that I've given you. Never be surprised when they ask you questions. Speak as you ought to speak. Trust My Holy Spirit for all answers.

Never be quick to speak. Listen to Me. You can't allow everyone around you. You are anointed to see, and speak everything that comes from Me. Again, always ask and trust Holy Spirit for what you see, speak, and dream.

You will be connected to others like you. Remember your new book. *The Secrets Are Out.* Nothing happens until the secrets are revealed! Don't think it's strange when people come in My name. Know the presence of the Angels: they come in My name. The are not strangers. They know who you are. You know who they are.

The sound is a sign to hear, listen, and do. Mediate on what you hear. Never fear. Visitation is here. It's your time. Invite them in. Always have your pen. You are a ready writer. Write the vision. Make it plain. It's all in My name. You see far. I've allowed you to top the bar.

Remember, Apostle recognized you were ready when he laid hands on you. He imparted what's on him to you. Now he's imparted in your husband what's on him. Be ye also ready for the task. We are ready for the task. We are seeing and speaking like never before.

We walk in opened doors. Doors we know and don't know. Sow, sow, sow. *The Ministry, Mission, of the Mystery is for our Mind, Marriage, and Money!* We have been released and recognized, for things we didn't see coming. Receive it all from Me! This is the Word from the Lord! Rejoice! Enjoy!

SEPTEMBER 25, 2016

It's Time to Wind and Dine in God's Divine!

I'm a Financial Witness and Financial Worker. Rivers of waters are overflowing, flooding, and flowing in my life with Financial Wealth, and Financial Wisdom. Money works for me. I tell money where and what to be. Money does what I tell it to do. Money is flowing and flooding in my life. It's raining money. I'm wet with money. Money has drenched me.

No more showers and shallow waters. I have stepped out into the deep. Money has overtaken me. Money has manifested to me. Money is flooding and flowing in my marriage and ministry. I see my money now. How it came, and when it started coming, I don't know.

I awakened to so much money that's constantly coming in my life. Money has been spoken out of my mouth. I decreed and I declared money to come to me. Money is where I want it to be — in my house.

I obeyed the prophet, Apostle Dr. Leroy Thompson. He said, "Money just keeps on coming to me." I just keep speaking. Money just keeps on coming to me. I stayed and I prayed. I asked God in Jesus name, and money came. I know things will never be the same.

Apostle Dr. Leroy Thompson laid hands on me. He said, "You are ready to receive." I received. All this money that just keeps on coming to me. I'm delivered, and divinely anointed and appointed to take money to its destinations. I sow seeds that have been ministered to me.

God is my source, sustainer, and supernatural supplier. I will never go back to lack or not enough. I can't even think broke again. I will never complain about money. My eyes are open. I see what's been promised and provided to me. I receive my prosperity. I'm living this life of a Financial Witness and Financial Worker. I live by this scripture.

> *For we are his workmanship, created in Christ Jesus unto good works, which God hath before ordained that we should walk in them.*
>
> Ephesians 2:10.

> *My light shines for all to see, as this scripture tells me. Let your light so shine before men, that they may see your good works, and glorify your Father which is in heaven.*
>
> Matthew 5:16 KJV

God's glory is revealed through me. Holy Spirit lives in and through me. The darkness is overtaken with the light that shines through me. People will see what marvelous work God has done, is doing, and continues to do, in and through me.

I'm happy. I'm rejoicing. I'm exceedingly glad. So much money. More money than I ever had. I obey God when He says sow. Good soil I will know. Holy Ghost is my helper. I will never be led wrong. This is where I belong. The crops have come up, because I'm God's very own. God allowed all this money to be shown. This is the Word from the Lord!

SEPTEMBER 26, 2016

Two arms in agreement, curved and connected together makes a heart. In the center is God. This makes God in their hearts. He's the center of the two. He allows you to be connected to Him. Holy Ghost is the connection point that makes the two come together and makes the connection with God. This heart can never be broke apart: because Holy Ghost made the connection and he's never the disconnection.

Never separate. God never makes a mistake. This connection is from the almighty, all-powerful God. Receive. Know your connection is from Me. This connection couldn't have been made without doing it in Jesus' name.

Always hear, listen, and do. Know who you are connected to. Stay connected. You shall have protection. You shall reap, receive, and rest in Me. Believe My prophet, who I have allowed to speak to thee. You shall receive always, your prosperity.

The stars are shinning bright. Innumerable stars. You can't count. Money with no particular amount. Unlimited. Receive. Again receive. All this money that has come from Me — blessings, after blessings. Blessed in spirit, health, and wealth, all in this order. They work together.

Without hearing from My Holy Spirit, you can't receive the wealth, without good health, you can't enjoy the wealth. These are three in one. The father, son, and Holy Spirit are three in one. I allow the mixing of the other two. Angels and you, and you shall know what to do. Know that having faith is the way. By grace, it's already done.

God wakes me early, to seek, after Him. These scripture tells me why.

> *I love them that love me; and those that seek me early shall find me.*
>
> Proverbs 8:17 KJV

> *And they rose early in the morning, and went forth into the wilderness of Tekoa: and as they went forth, Jehoshaphat stood and said, Hear me, O Judah, and ye inhabitants of Jerusalem; Believe in the Lord your God, so shall ye be established; believe his prophets, so shall ye prosper.*
>
> 2 Chronicles 20:20 KJV

> *If ye abide in me, and my words abide in you, ye shall ask what ye will, and it shall be done unto you.*
>
> John 15:7 KJV

Rising early and going forth, speaking and hearing, believing God and being established allows you to believe His prophets, which gives you prosperity. Never cease to seek Him early. Awake and make no mistake. Hear and believe who God has sent your way. Know this is what God has to say. When you obey, blessings of prosperity shall continue to come to you every day in every way. This is the Word from the Lord!

October

OCTOBER 2, 2016

The comforter and counselor has come to take complete control of you. He never misses a Moment to help you. Blessings after blessings continue to take over you. God has saved the best for last. Your future is greater than your past. God's plans have come to prosper you. Follow through.

Big and enormous blessings have come to you. I receive all these promises given me. Hear and listen to the heartbeat. God has laid it all at your feet.

Always hear the sound. This sound brings the abundance to you. This sound brings the wisdom to you. This sound brings the health and wealth to you. There's a message in the sound. Know that God is around. Praise Him with the sound of loud instruments. Praise Him with a loud shout. God has brought you out.

Walls have come down with a sound. Speaking out is a sound — the sound of ministering angels. Hear, listen, and do what has been spoken to you. Mysteries are revealed from the sound.

Praying in the Spirit. Hear the sound of God's voice. Make a joyful noise unto the Lord. There's releasing in the noise. Listen carefully to what you hear. He's in the atmosphere. Short sounds, loud and long sounds. Trumpets have sounded. Horns blown. Sounds known and unknown.

Holy Spirit releases what's meant to be. He's never wrong. Continue in song. Sing loud and sing low, just sing out and be not silent. It's still a sound.

What God speaks has come, and shall continue to come to pass. You must know the sound. The voice of Holy Spirit speaks and continues to speak to you. Never go your way. Always remember what God has to say overrules what you want to say.

Move in the moment, continue to praise and worship God in Spirit and in truth. Never do what you want to do. Open the door. It's here. Again, receive.

Never leave this place. Place of wealth and riches that has come to your house. This place of spiritual-minded life and peace. This place of purpose God has called you to.

Speak to the people, and compel them to come. Tell them to come away from the place they've been delivered from. The sound shall always be. Listen to what has come from Me. I am your almighty, all-powerful, awesome God. This is the Word from the Lord!

OCTOBER 3, 2016

Lord I love you with all my heart. In you I will never depart. You loved me from the start. You are never far. Thank you, Lord, for loving me. I am your beloved one. Thank you for what you've done. In Christ Jesus, I have won. Thank you for your Son.

I keep going and going, even when the road gets rough. I get tough. I'm on Your mind. You have my mind all the time. I never get tired in this race. You have placed me here for Jesus' sake.

I keep my eye on the prize. In Christ Jesus, I rise. Higher and higher I go, wherever You say to go, even when I don't know. I make moves in the spirit because You have given me Your Holy Spirit. I receive.

Everything you want me to be. I become. Victory after victory I've won. When I arise every day, I say thank you. Each day I praise and pray to You, my heavenly and earthly father. I follow you in all that I do. I speak, and seek you continually.

Oh how I love You so. My heart does magnify You in all I do and continue to do. My mind is in line, with You, because You are divine and You allow me to shine. The light is on, never to go dim or dark. I'm in this moment of your presence. Never to leave, because I believe, and I receive all that You have already and keep giving me. Blessings after blessings, never ending.

Praise has made a way out of no way. You are bigger than any situations or circumstances that try to block or stop you. You are the greatest! I stretch and reach for the unreachable. *You have placed, positioned, and provided all these promises to prosper me, because it pleases You to prosper me.* I thank you and I thank you, over and over again. In Christ Jesus, I win. This is the Word from the Lord!

OCTOBER 11, 2016

Word received in Baton Rouge

I receive all Your Word spoken around me. As far as the east from the west, so we are flowing in Your best. This was supposed to happen. Receive in My presence, brand new revelations today. Take all that has been given to you. Never be ashamed to receive in My name. Share the Word you have heard. Call those things that are not as though they were.

Word read from prayer warrior

> *And it shall be to me a name of joy, a praise and an honour before all the nations of the earth, which shall hear all the good that I do unto them: and they shall fear and tremble for all the goodness and for all the prosperity that I procure unto it.*
>
> Jeremiah 33:9 KJV

You are out. Never return. These blessings you didn't earn, you learned. You are trained in Jesus' name. You are home in what you own. Everywhere you go, flow in blessings you didn't know. Go, grow, glow, and continue to sow.

Always listen to the sound. God is always around. Small sounds and big sounds, there's blessings in the noise. Make a joyful noise always.

In the lands you are walking, you are in My plans. It is written that the enemy is smitten. Hear Me, and you know what to do. My blessings are on you.

Praise Me with a song and dance. All the blessings are in your hands. Keep dancing and praising, you are out, shout, shout, shout. I made all this money come about. Listen to the loud-sounding instruments. Receive what you see it's all from Me. Obey what I say in the sound.

Receive revelations that have been revealed and continue to keep coming from Me. This is the Word from God!

OCTOBER 19, 2016

You made a way out of no way. Love like never before. People come from everywhere. The lost have been found. You always remind people of the sound. Listening to God's voice is a choice. Hear, listen, and do what He says to do. It's up to you.

Money is dropping like bombs. Exploding. Coming from everywhere. People giving to you. Past money, present money, future money that keeps on coming.

Break out of money. Like a disease breaks out. Spreading of money. Released money. Found money. Money that has found you, and you know what to do. It's supernaturally supplied, multiplied to you. Never-ending money. Plenty money. No stress, struggle or strain. Money remains.

Jumping money. Money in leaps and bounds to reach you. Stretching money — when you thought you would run out, more money was brought about. Shout!

Screaming money. Speaking loud money. Money isn't silent; it makes a statement. People will say, "Look at what God has done." Seeing money, that's no longer a mystery. No longer hidden. Money's revealed.

Healing money. No longer sick of being held back from you. No lack of money. Exceedingly, abundantly, above all that you could have asked or thought about.

Kingdom money. Kingdom missions. Kingdom ministry and marriage. Money that never miscarriages. Money you never lose. Money you must choose. How much do you want money. Never forget the mission of your money. Enjoy money. Seed-sowing money. Keep sowing and you will keep receiving your harvest. The harvest won't come without the seeds sown.

Keep the love flowing. Keep growing and going. Love from the heart and God will never depart.

Plant your seed.
Pat your soil.
Prepare for the supernatural.

Receive. Receive. Receive. All this money coming from Me. I am the almighty, all-powerful God of all. This is the Word from God!

OCTOBER 26, 2016

God is sending us to our new church location. We will pastor a few hundred at first because God wants to show us what He has and can do through us obeying Him. Because you detoured you delayed the process. Now you are back on track there can be no turning back.

God wants to show off in us. People will see what He has done. It's not about where *we* wanted to be, it's where *He* wants us to be. He knows we know how to do things His way. He will show off in us.

Thousands we will pastor, it's a must. People must understand in God we trust. God had to show us it's His way and not ours. The light affliction was only for a moment, however it seemed longer. We had to learn lessons in the testing.

We must never return to the vomit. Know that we are responsible. If we had known this before time, we might have got back out of line. We are here to stay and continue to do things God's way, and know that there's no other way. People are blessed because of our obedience.

We Teach the Scriptures.
Train the Saints.
Trust the Savior.

Live in the abundant life, where your anointing flows freely. Always access the power and authority, live, walk, and work in miracles, manifestations and plenty of money. This is the word from God!

OCTOBER 29, 2016

When we close our eyes and mediate on our God-given purpose, we picture in our minds where we will soon be and what we will become. We see the first picture, however don't stop at what we see at first, continue to the next and next pictures until we get to the end of what we see in our minds. That's where God wants us to be at that particular time. We must see beyond the sight.

The enemy tries to stop us with the first good thing we see. God says, "Obey Me and you will be all I've promised you to be." Remember your stops along the way; however never stop because your steps are ordered day by day. Your mind is renewed every day, so why would you stop at what you see today? We must always obey.

Chart, channel, continue and correct your thoughts. What you think and see is important. Chart what you see, write it down because these thoughts might now stay around. Channel your thoughts, make sure they go in the right direction. You set the course.

Continue your thoughts. You have unlimited flow of where God wants you to go. Correct what's not in line with God's divine. Shine each time, as you remember each step and stop along the way to your divine destined destination, God has promised, provided, and is pleased to prosper you!

Receive what you see from Me. I am that I am. I am your almighty, all-powerful God. God has spoken!

November

NOVEMBER 22, 2016

Thanksgiving and Gratefulness

Keep showing compassion and loving on people because your kind words, hugs, and kisses, might be the very thing that will help someone pick themselves up. Your love closes up holes that will prevent others from falling in the ditch. Always be thankful, even when things don't go the way you want them to go at that time. Keep being grateful.

Your time of manifestation will come, because it's already been done by grace through faith, God has made and continues to make a way out of no way. God's blessings are here to stay: they are immeasurable and unlimited.

When you continue in thanksgiving and gratefulness, you will continue in love and compassion, knowing that nothing can stop what God has allowed to come about. Always be ready to give a soft answer, kind words, and have good thoughts to think all these things. This is why we should be thankful and grateful. When we are full of these two, God says, "What do you want Me to do for you?"

Live life, love life, love to laugh, enjoy the best life, receiving blessings that you never had. Why? This place and position in life makes God glad. It's His pleasure to prosper us! Give thanks with a grateful heart, because of what God has done. He's given you His only begotten Son. This is the victory we have won. When you know what it is to win, losing is never an option. Keep your mind on the winner's side.

Know that God always provides. This is God's Thanksgiving and Gratefulness message. Receive. Obey. There are more manifestations of bountiful blessings on the way. Rejoice and be exceedingly glad. God will continue to manifest prosperity that you never had. This is the word of the Lord!

NOVEMBER 24, 2016

Listening and Recognizing Sounds

>Sound sleep
>Shower spraying
>Surrendering saint
>Souls saved
>Spiritual speaking
>Sending signals
>Supernatural surplus

Shortage isn't an option. Sow seeds of sacrifice for the supernatural. Sow stretch seeds, and special seeds. Seeds that make you say wow, because you didn't know how. You obeyed what you heard. See the manifestations of your seeds sown. You have grown. That's what My seed says. Seeds talk. Seeds take you higher and higher.

Listen to the sound of the seeds. Seeds never sleep, because they are planted for you to reap. Seeds don't need showering and spraying, they need watering just right, to bring what you are saying. Pay attention to the sounds, there's always a message in what you hear. If you don't understand at first, don't fear. Know that angels are near.

Wait for Holy Spirit to reveal. He gives you the wisdom, knowledge and understanding of what you hear. Sounds are heard on the outside, but brought from the inside. You accept what you hear from your mind giving you the knowledge of the sound.

You have heard birds chirping before, so you recognize the sound. You've heard your parents' voice, so you know who's talking or calling you, even when you don't see them. Words are important. Even though you don't see

Me, your almighty God, by My Words you know that I'm speaking to you by way of Holy Spirit.

Music playing and dancing, and then silence. There are good sounds and there are what we call bad sounds. Remember all sounds have a message to the hearer. We determine what the sound is and what we do when we hear it. Make a joyful noise unto the Lord. Rejoice and be exceedingly glad.

Shout unto the Lord with the voice of triumph. Thank the Lord for sounds. Thank the Lord you can hear sounds. Praise Him with Psalms and hymns and spiritual songs making melody in your heart as unto the Lord. Thank Him because it's already done.

What you've said, and heard, it's a sound. When we believe God's prophets, so shall we prosper. There is a blessing in the sound, the voice of the prophet. Receive, because shortage isn't an option. We must hear, listen, and do what God has spoken, is speaking, and continues to speak. Hear these words from the Lord!

December

DECEMBER 13, 2016

Hear these words and allow them to be you.

1) Calm
2) Confident
3) Consistent
4) Compassionate
5) Continue

When we stay *Calm* and don't panic in the things God has chosen and told us to do, we will remain *Confident and Consistent*, receiving and knowing God has already provided, promised, and allowed everything to come to pass in our lives. We must be *Compassionate and Continue* to pray, and praise without *ceasing*, knowing our God has promoted and given us prosperity, all because this gives Him pleasure when we prosper.

Never give up on God, even when the dust hasn't settled and the wind is continually blowing the obstacles your way. Know that obstacles are moving because of the wind and dust blowing. God has turned them into dominion and divine destinations. Remember the rushing mighty wind in this scripture:

> *And suddenly there came a sound from heaven as of a rushing mighty wind, and it filled all the house where they were sitting. And there appeared unto them cloven tongues like as of fire, and it sat upon each of them. And they were all filled with the Holy Ghost, and began to speak with other tongues, as the Spirit gave them utterance.*
>
> *And it shall come to pass in the last days, saith God, I will pour out of my Spirit upon all flesh: and your sons and your daughters shall prophesy, and your young men shall see visions, and your old men shall dream dreams: And on my servants and on my handmaidens I will pour out in those days of my Spirit; and they shall prophesy: And I will shew wonders in heaven above, and signs in the earth beneath; blood, and fire, and vapour of smoke:*
>
> *And it shall come to pass, that whosoever shall call on the name of the Lord shall be saved.*
>
> Acts 2:2-4, 17-19, 21 KJV

Know that even though the wind blows, God continues to show off in and through you. He's already done, and continues to do through you, by way of Holy Spirit that's in you. Greater works you shall do and continue to do because you are called and chosen for the tasks. Your blessings shall always last. Unlimited, supernatural supply, they continue to multiply. Receive!!!

> *For we are God's [own] handiwork (His workmanship), recreated in Christ Jesus, [born anew] that we may do those good works which God predestined (planned beforehand) for us [taking paths which He prepared ahead of time], that we should walk in them [living the good life which He prearranged and made ready for us to live].*
>
> Ephesians 2:10AMPC

DECEMBER 17, 2016

Because of what you went through, I've increased your giving and your living. Never decrease the seeds you sow, and you shall continue to receive divine supernatural surplus. Enjoy life and be happy in Christ Jesus. He's the reason for the abundant life you're living.

Rejoice and be exceedingly glad. The heavens are open. Receive on earth what's been released from heaven. The angels are busy working on your behalf, bringing all things from Me to pass.

The gates are open. You have asked for Big! Doors are not an option to walk in: because they are too small. Gates are large. This is the large place I've set you in. Receive. Walk in. Keep moving. Never stop working and walking in wisdom and wealth.

You are a sign and a wonder. I've worked miracles for you, in you, and through you. Your work is complete only when the end comes. Your end is far off. You live long and strong. You are strong in Me and in the power of My might. Love and Live right. Always do what's right in My sight. It's never your fight. It's always your victory. Your enemies are destroyed. Always allow

Me to do My part, and I shall never depart as long as you keep doing things from the heart.

> *And he said, Hearken ye, all Judah, and ye inhabitants of Jerusalem, and thou king Jehoshaphat, Thus saith the Lord unto you, Be not afraid nor dismayed by reason of this great multitude; for the battle is not yours, but God's.*
>
> *Ye shall not need to fight in this battle: set yourselves, stand ye still, and see the salvation of the Lord with you, O Judah and Jerusalem: fear not, nor be dismayed; to morrow go out against them: for the Lord will be with you.*
>
> 2 Chronicles 20:15, 17 KJV

I have removed, rescued, and released, you from the riots. Receive everything I have reserved and restored for you to prosper. I promised, I did it, and shall continue to do it. It's My pleasure to give **IT** to you. Increase and Treasures from heaven — unlimited blessings. You heard it from Me.

Harvest time is here. Have no fear. I'm always near. I never leave or forsake you. Continue to do as I chosen, commanded, commissioned, and charged you to do. Keep moving. Nothing can be activated without movement.

When I spoke to darkness in the beginning it moved away and light moved in. Since manifestations and money have moved in, lack and little has moved out. Remember, I made it all come about. Praise Me with a shout.

Shouting is important. Enemies were defeated with a shout. Walls came down with a shout. Triumph came with a shout.

> *O clap your hands, all ye people; shout unto God with the voice of triumph.*
>
> *He shall subdue the people under us, and the nations under our feet.*
>
> Psalms 47:1, 3 KJV

And it shall come to pass, that when they make a long blast with the ram's horn, and when ye hear the sound of the trumpet, all the people shall shout with a great shout; and the wall of the city shall fall down flat, and the people shall ascend up every man straight before him.

Joshua 6:5 KJV

DECEMBER 29, 2016

The Heart Condition

Eight Important Keys To His Kingdom:

1) Marriage Clean

2) Mission Clear

3) Ministry Compassion

4) Motives Correct

5) Mind Changed

6) Made Connections

7) Money Coming

8) Manifestations Continuing

God has given these **Eight Important Keys To His Kingdom.** Everything we do, as believers, must be based on having **The Heart Condition** from God. Our focus has to be this: See what He wants to get from, through, and to me. It's all about you, me, and Him. We must allow God to continue to help us bring them — them being the lost souls — to His Kingdom, which lasts forever.

This Heart Condition has Holy Ghost Help. It's filled with the right blood, Jesus' Blood. It never misses a rhythm or beat. Because of the sound, our enemies He defeats. The world looks at its condition as being bad, but God sees it as receiving blessings we never had.

This Heart Condition is the good condition for the mission. Everything we do must be from the condition of our hearts. We must love right and live right in His sight.

> *Those who lead blameless lives and do what is right, speaking the truth from sincere hearts.*
>
> Psalms 15:2 NLT

What we see, what people see, must be what God sees through the condition of our hearts.

> *The law of his God is in his heart; none of his steps shall slide.*
>
> Psalm 37:31 AMPC

1) Marriage Clean

In marriage, we must function together in love, be in agreement and work as one flesh. We leave father and mother, sticking and staying close to each other. This is the first and foremost important key to **The Heart Condition**. Without it nothing else can come.

> *So they are no longer two, but one flesh. What therefore God has joined together, let not man put asunder (separate).*
>
> Matthew 19:6 AMPC

> *For this reason a man shall leave his father and his mother and shall be joined to his wife, and the two shall become one flesh. [Gen. 2:24.]*
>
> Ephesians 5:31 AMPC

Here's a very important **K.E.Y.** (Kept Equally Yolked) that God has given me. Know your spouse. Husbands must know they have **favor in the find. A wife is a true treasure to find.**

Do not be unequally yoked with unbelievers [do not make mismated alliances with them or come under a different yoke with them, inconsistent with your faith]. For what partnership have right living and right standing with God with iniquity and lawlessness? Or how can light have fellowship with darkness?

2 Corinthians 6:14 AMPC

The man who finds a wife finds a treasure, and he receives favor from the LORD.

Proverbs 18:22 NLT

Like-minded, having love for each other. Never turning to others for what you are legally bonded, signed and sealed to do together, sexually and emotionally.

Let marriage be held in honor (esteemed worthy, precious, of great price, and especially dear) in all things. And thus let the marriage bed be undefiled (kept undishonored); for God will judge and punish the unchaste [all guilty of sexual vice] and adulterous.

Hebrews 13:4 AMPC

2) Mission Clear

This is knowing our God-given purpose in life. We work the process and follow through with the procedures according to His plans, and then we can ultimately make it to the finish line of where our faith has taken us. We must know who we are, and who He's allowed us to be connected with to achieve and **receive the goals of grace that have already been given to us by the finish line of faith.** This is the only way that we can then function together in

3) Ministry Compassion

Where we keep loving and working for God with our

4) Motives Correct

Having Holy Ghost's help, and a daily renewed mind, God thoughts, and

5) Mind Changed

To do and be all that God has fitly joined, perfectly made and designed us to be, operating in His perfect will for our lives. We must know without a doubt He has brought us out. Shout! **We can't have the wrong mindset.** We gotta know we are His best, made to do better than the rest. **We can't receive what we haven't believed. Nothing happens except God reveals His secrets to His servants the prophets. They speak what He says, not what they want to say.**

6) Made Connections

These connections must be made from God, allowing Holy Ghost to speak to, through, and for us. We must know how to hear what Holy Spirit speaks to our spirit, and say what He says, and keep saying, keep praying, keep praising, keep preaching, and keep prophesying. These made connections are for our training, teaching, and treasures. They are to help us receive

7) Money Coming

That keeps on coming to us as God has already preserved, positioned, promised and provided these

8) Manifestations Continuing

To come, as He allows His prophets to speak, and we believe what **they say because of what God said in His word** in this scripture:

> *And they rose early in the morning and went out into the Wilderness of Tekoa; and as they went out, Jehoshaphat stood and said, Hear me, O Judah, and you inhabitants of Jerusalem! Believe in the Lord your God and you*

shall be established; believe and remain steadfast to His prophets and you shall prosper.

2 Chronicles 20:20 AMPC

God wants us to receive His prosperity, because this gives Him pleasure. We want God to be pleased in all we do for Him and His people. He called us for this particular reason, to operate in this season. Our hearts must pump and beat to the rhythm of Holy Spirit which gives us wisdom, word and wealth as **we receive from the source, (God) His resources, reminders, and we remain, in Christ Jesus. Know that this Heart Condition He's allowed us to obtain.**

DECEMBER 30, 2016

T.I.D.E.

Goal Hands Up

1) Trash Incinerator Dissolves Everything
2) Treasure Increase Dominion Everyday
3) Triumph Impartation Deliverance Eternally

Goal Hands Up

TOUCH DOWN

Anything that's outside of the left or right of the goal won't make it to what's Under-the-line, which is **TOUCH DOWN**

The T.I.D.E. is coming. Be ready. Wow! **This large wave is here.** The T.I.D.E. had to come before the wave; it's here now. God is near. You had to be ready before it came. Are you ready in Jesus' mighty name? *Yes or no?* Let's go.

God has moved all things from you for a show. Your life will never be the same. His desire for you is to shine in His divine at all times.

1) Trash Incinerator Dissolve Everything.

2) Treasures Increase Dominion Everyday.

God has allowed His blessings to flow anyway. You have received because of His love, your love, and your obedience to Him only. Because of this, you have received,

3) Triumph Impartation Deliverance Eternally.

You have received these things because abundance is your birthright. "You must love Me with all your might," says the almighty, all-powerful God of all. This is for those that will hear, listen, and do all that's required of you.

Never be afraid of the wave. You have brand new mercies every day. Watch and continue to see and receive this large body of water that continues to flow and flood all for His show. Where or how it was formed is not your concern. God's Spirit you must discern. You must know that you've earned.

This **T.I.D.E. is from the asking. You asked, God delivered. Now, you are dominating. Receive. No, more questions to ask.** These blessings shall last. **Touch down. Now!** Even when you don't know how. God allowed it all to come about. He has brought you out.

From dry and dessert places, to wet and wonderful promises. You have provisions, promotions, and prosperity Now! Enjoy! It's My pleasure! This is the Word from God!

DECEMBER 31, 2016

Sow, sow, sow, and receive blessings you didn't even know. Your seeds allow you to receive all these blessings that have come upon thee. **Plant your**

seed in the right soils, and you will receive the real crops. *Artificial is a form of the real thing.*

> *Having a form of godliness, but denying the power thereof: from such turn away.*
>
> 2 Timothy 3:5 KJV

Why receive a form of when you can receive from above! (Heaven). Let heaven be your portion. **Receive your supply.** *Never accept just getting by. This is the year you shall receive! Stay Clean and Receive Everything in 2017!*

Where to sow, you will know. God has set it all up for you to grow. **Supernatural seeds have been given, for a supernatural harvest. Crops have come up. Receive. This word I shall continue to speak. Receive. Receive. Receive. It's important to start receiving.** *Remember to continue to sow seeds.* The harvest has come, because it's His will being done, right here on earth as it is in heaven.

The heavens are open. The large gates are open. God has set you in this large place, for Jesus Christ's sake. His Kingdom wins, in 2017.

There's nothing you will ever need that He hasn't already provided. There's nothing you will ever want for that He hasn't already opened the door for. **Walk through. It's been given you.**

When you prosper, God's Kingdom prospers. **Wealth and riches are in your house. Receive.** Mansions, houses, and land — it's all in His plans. **Receive.**

Marriages renewed. Receive. Ministries restored. Receive. Money just keeps on coming. Receive. You know your **Mission. Receive.** Nothing is impossible. **Receive.** *Anything that tries or look impossible don't receive.* Know that God has already made it possible. **Receive.**

"Any way that you can't see, keep your eyes enlighten on Me," says the almighty, all-powerful God of all. **Whoever obeys what He has said and continues to say,** know that He shall keep these blessings coming your way, every day. **Receive.**

> *Never speak what you don't want, but always speak what you want. Speak what God speaks.* **Receive what He says.** *Remember love, live life from the heart. If you do this, God will never depart.*
>
> *A good person produces good things from the treasury of a good heart, and an evil person produces evil things from the treasury of an evil heart. What you say flows from what is in your heart.*
>
> Luke 6:45 NLT

He sees from the heart, the inward man, which He renews daily. Bring everything from the heart daily. You shall stay clean and receive everything in 2017. Receive.

CONCLUSION

As this year of 2017 approaches, hear what God has spoken. God spoke these words. **Staying Clean and Receive Everything in 2017.** God explains it this way in this scripture. Let's read it.

> *If you keep yourself pure, you will be a special utensil for honorable use. Your life will be clean, and you will be ready for the Master to use you for every good work.*
>
> 2 Timothy 2:21 NLT

What an awesome God! Will you receive? I receive. Continue to pray, and praise Him. As I have written, I can hardly wait for you to receive what God has spoken to me. ***The Secrets Are Out,*** **will bless His people and all those who will obey what He has said, says, and continues to say.** *It's a must that we obey. God's Word spoken will help fix the broken.* See what He says in this scripture.

The Spirit of the LORD is upon me, for he has anointed me to bring Good News to the poor. He has sent me to proclaim that captives will be released, that the blind will see, that the oppressed will be set free,

Luke 4:18 NLT

I know you will be blessed. This is why: God has already done it by grace, through faith. Again speak what He says, do it His way. Love Him with all your might, mind, and live right all the time. Make sure your motive is love in all you do. He first loved you. You are His beloved. He's displayed His love, in giving you His only begotten Son.

The victory over all has been won. Be blessed. Enjoy!

I decree and declare, I believe God's prophets, therefore I receive my prosperity!

About the Author

Lady Mary Hatter is a wife, mother, grandmother, renowned author, entrepreneur, and Co-Founder of Kingdom Minded Church along with her husband Pastor AD Hatter. Lady Mary is the Founder of GCW God's C.H.A.S.E.D. Women. She's the author of several books; which her very first book, she received a Literary Award from the Association of Independent Ministries, Founded by Bishop IV and Lady Bridget Hilliard. Lady Mary has a love and passion for helping to bring lost souls into the Kingdom of God. She understands that this pleases God when we walk in our purpose of The Great Commission as explained in this scripture:

> *Jesus came and told his disciples, I have been given all authority in heaven and on earth.*
>
> *Therefore, go and make disciples of all the nations, baptizing them in the name of the Father and the Son and the Holy Spirit.*
>
> *Teach these new disciples to obey all the commands I have given you. And be sure of this: I am with you always, even to the end of the age.*

Matthew 28:18-20 NLT

She is anointed and appointed by God to teach and preach His Word, so that the lost can be found, and the saved never loose their sound; this voice to cry out loud and spare not. She gives God all she got. God has blessed her with the prophetic anointing to speak His secrets; which are His Words, to His body of baptized believers. He has imparted, instructed, and inspired her to live wholeheartedly for Him. Lady Mary knows that when she seeks first the kingdom of God and His righteousness, He adds all things unto her. See below:

But seek ye first the kingdom of God, and his righteousness; and all these things shall be added unto you.

Matthew 6:33 KJV

If you enjoyed reading

The Secrets Are Out,

please leave a brief review on

Amazon and Goodreads

to help spread the word.

Thank you ~ Lady Mary Hatter

Bonus Content

What are Decrees?

I'm glad you asked.

5 Things about Decrees

1) We always decree out loud.

2) Decree is about authority.

3) Decrees help establish God's will on the earth through those who decree and declare His Word.

4) When we decree prosperity, we cut in half and slice poverty with a two-edged sword.

5) When we decree a thing, Holy Ghost fire burns on earth and causes God's glory and plans to be manifested.

What the scripture says about Decrees:

Thou shalt also decree a thing, and it shall be established unto thee: and the light shall shine upon thy ways.

Job 22:28 KJV

Death and life are in the power of the tongue: and they that love it shall eat the fruit thereof.

Proverbs 18:21 KJV

In other words you shall possess that which you speak. Let's Decree some things and command our angels to work on our behalf.

10 Decrees and Declares

1) I decree and declare that the supply of heaven is my portion.

2) I decree and declare that the supply of heaven has swallowed up and devoured all my lack.

3) I decree and declare that with my mouth I carve out a realm of prosperity as I speak blessings and favor in Jesus' name.

4) I decree and declare that God is always with me.

5) I decree and declare that my days of breakthrough are over because I've broken through.

6) I decree and declare that anything that has held me back in the past has been defeated. I receive my victory now.

7) I decree and declare that my faith has increased and I speak to mountains and they are removed.

8) I decree and declare I'm walking in the abundance that God has given me.

9) I decree and declare that anything from my past that tries or has tried to derail my victory is defeated destroyed and covered by the blood of Jesus.

10) I decree and declare that my season of frustration and lack is over and I have stepped into and I supernatural time travel into all that God has for me in Jesus' name, and I will go everywhere and proclaim that Jesus Christ is Lord.

The 25 Decrees and Declarations of My Soul

1) I decree and declare: I am available to God, obeying, and keeping His commandments.

2) I decree and declare: I am anchored in my soul, and the money keeps on coming to me.

3) I decree and declare: I am anointed to prosper, and receive my prosperity now.

4) I decree and declare: I am in alignment spiritually with my mind, and my soul.

5) I decree and declare: I am in divine agreement with God and man, and am receiving God's promises.

6) I decree and declare: I am advancing to higher levels and I have power over devils.

7) I decree and declare: I am training my soul and receiving blessings untold.

8) I decree and declare: I am renewing my mind and what I speak out of my mouth is in line.

9) I decree and declare: I am keeping my mind and soul in Christ Jesus, knowing he rose for this very reason — our Salvation.

10) I decree and declare: I am speaking what God says and receiving my harvest.

11) I decree and declare: I am always thanking God and receiving all from Him.

12) I decree and declare: I am magnifying God with my soul and receiving my blessings as they unfold.

13) I decree and declare: I am working the process and receiving my possessions.

14) I decree and declare: I am living in the Kingdom of God and I have kingdom keys.

15) I decree and declare: I am unlocking all financial doors from God, walking through them, and receiving everything.

16) I decree and declare: I am turning the keys to my blessings and my miracle keys are working.

17) I decree and declare: I am unlocking myself of all debt.

18) I decree and declare: I am free of debt and I have broken my net.

19) I decree and declare: I am living in my due seasons, receiving for myself, and kingdom reasons.

20) I decree and declare: I am marked for greatness and I receive greatness now.

21) I decree and declare: I am living in righteousness, in rest, and receiving revelations every day.

22) I decree and declare: I am living by grace through faith and receiving everything God has sent my way.

23) I decree and declare: I am abundantly supplied and my money is multiplied.

24) I decree and declare: I am receiving all my blessings.

25) I decree and declare: I am exceedingly glad and living a great life of love and laughter.

I pray and I stay until God allows everything to come my way. I shall never go astray, because I know it's God who's already made the way. I receive all His promises today. Satan and his army can never take them away.

What I decree and declare has come to pass, and shall always last. Now, I have more blessings than I ever had. I receive all these blessings that have come upon me because of my God and speaking His Decrees of prosperity.

Key Notes!!!

Praying in the Holy Ghost activates and allows me to access what God has already done for me.

God, I'm praying in the Holy Ghost for you to show me how to receive… whatever you're praying for or asking for.

12 SR's from God!
1) Show me how to receive all the blessings you have already given me.

2) Show me what to do to receive more of and from you.

3) Show me when and where you want me to go, and not where I think I know.

4) Show me what I have to do to stay in right standing with you.

5) Show me who you have sent for me to listen to.

6) Show me who has your heart and has been set apart to help me go far.

7) Reveal and expose what you want me to see.

8) Remove and let die so that my fruits multiply.

9) Revive in me what you want to come alive in me.

10) Restore what you want me to receive more of.

11) Reassign and realign my life into what you want it to be.

12) Renew, review, and make brand new in me, so that I can do everything you want me to do, and receive everything that only comes from you by way of Holy Spirit. This way is for sure, period.

3) Show me when and where you want me to go, and not where I think I know.

4) Show me what I have to do to stay in right standing with you.

5) Show me who you have sent for me to listen to.

6) Show me who has your heart and has been set apart to help me go far.

7) Reveal and expose what you want me to see.

8) Remove and let die so that my fruits multiply.

9) Revive in me what you want to come alive in me.

10) Restore what you want me to receive more of.

11) Reassign and realign my life into what you want it to be.

12) Renew, review, and make brand new in me, so that I can do everything you want me to do, and receive everything that only comes from you by way of Holy Spirit. This way is for sure, period.

www.ingramcontent.com/pod-product-compliance
Lightning Source LLC
Chambersburg PA
CBHW070113080526
44586CB00013B/1277